Live like your life is hanging by a thread — because once, it was. And we didn't let go.

Quang Ma

Life Hanging by a Thread

A Vietnamese Refugee Family's

Journey of Fear, Faith

and Freedom

Quang Ma

For permission requests, contact the author at:
lifehangingbyathread@yahoo.com

First published in the United States of America, 2026

Published by Quang Ma Publishing Loma Linda, California

ISBN (Paperback): 979-8-9951151-0-6

ASIN (eBook): B0GL8YQ2YZ

Library of Congress Control Number: 2026907969

Printed in the United States of America

10 9 8 7 6 5 4 3 2 1

Disclaimer

This is a work of nonfiction based on the author's personal experiences and memories. Events have been reconstructed to the best of the author's recollection. Some names and identifying details have been changed to protect the privacy of individuals. The author has made every effort to ensure accuracy, but acknowledges that memory is imperfect and others who lived through these events may recall them differently.

DEDICATION

To my mother and father, whose courage, sacrifice and endurance carried our family through every uncertainty, fear and unimaginable hardship

TABLE OF CONTENTS

Title page iii

Copyright iv

Dedication v

Table of Contents...vii

Prologue ix

Map of Vietnam...xi

Chapter 1 — The Fall and Fragile Sanctuary 1

Chapter 2 — The Great Flood..5

Chapter 3 — Where the Dream Took Root.......................................9

Chapter 4 — The First to Go 15

Chapter 5 — Preparing to Leave.. 19

Chapter 6 — Learning the Compass and the Map.......................23

Chapter 7 — My Escape – Just a Little Tour 27

Chapter 8 — The First Night in the Ocean 31

Chapter 9 — The Engine Died at 1 PM...35

Chapter 10 — The Ship That Turned Back 39

Chapter 11 — Singapore – The First Safe Ground....................... 51

Chapter 12 — Bataan: The Waiting Island...................................55

Chapter 13 — America – The First Morning of a New Life............ 61

Chapter 14 — Walton High School – Bronx, New York (1985)........65

Chapter 15 — A Second Family in Upstate New York....................69

Chapter 16 — My Father's Escape – The Fourteen-Day Ordeal.......73

Chapter 17 — The Escape by Land – Phượng and Út's Journey
            Through Cambodia to Thailand 87

Chapter 18 — Settling In – Learning, Working, and the Early
American Years 97

Chapter 19 — University – Where the Dream Became Reality (1989–1996) 101

Chapter 20 —The Turtle at Midnight 107

Chapter 21 — One Phone Call Away (1997–2001) 115

Chapter 22 — The Day the Dream Became Whole......................... 123

Chapter 23 — The Years We Learned to Love Again 127

Chapter 24 — Pat and Brian...131

Chapter 25 — The Quiet Strength of My Parents........................... 139

Chapter 26 — Two Stories from VA Hospital................................. 145

Chapter 27 — Letters to My Son 143

Chapter 28 — The Price of Freedom..155

A Tribute to Phượng... 159

A Tribute to Ánh... 163

A Tribute to Thành 167

Epilogue — Faith That Carried Us Home................................... 171

Acknowledgments...175

About the Author 177

PROLOGUE

ix

When South Vietnam fell on April 30, 1975, the war ended, but the suffering did not.

Reeducation camps, forced labor, and silent fear settled over every family. Homes were taken. Fields no longer belonged to those who worked them. Many were sent to distant "new economic zones"—remote places with little food and no future. In just a few months, a lifetime of hard work disappeared.

Freedom was slowly stripped away. Education, jobs, and even daily choices came under strict control. Speaking the wrong word could lead to prison. Sentences lasted for decades. When people finally walked out, they had lost more than time. They had lost their lives as they once knew them.

People did not leave for adventure. They left because they had no choice.

They risked everything on the sea—storms, pirates, hunger, and death—all for one simple thing: the chance to live without fear.

To learn.
To work.
To speak.
To raise children with dreams.

This is not only my story.
It is the story of more than one million Vietnamese who crossed oceans and borders, carrying nothing but hope.

And it begins with a ten-year-old boy who did not yet know what was coming.

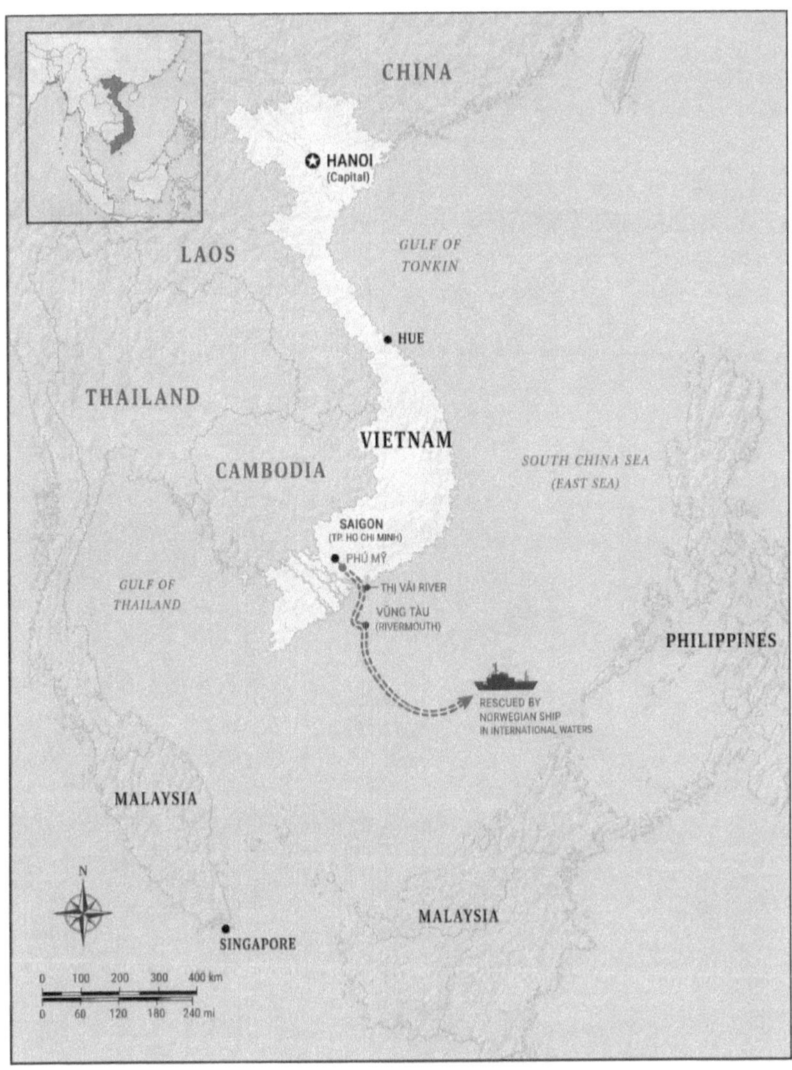

1984, My Escape Route from Phú Mỹ to International Waters

Chapter 1

THE FALL AND FRAGILE SANCTUARY

The world I knew did not end with a single explosion. It ended quietly, in the way everything familiar slowly disappeared.

I was ten years old when South Vietnam fell on April 30, 1975.

At that age, I did not fully understand what it meant for a country to lose a war. I only knew that something heavy, something dark, had slipped into our lives. The adults whispered urgently, packed their belongings in silence at night, and constantly glanced over their shoulders, as if danger were always just behind them.

We lived in Bình Tuy, a quiet town near a military base where my father worked as an administrative officer. My mother sold rice at the local market two kilometers away, walking the same familiar path every morning, her basket balanced against the early mist. Together, they were raising six children, with more on the way.

In April 1975, rumors spread faster than the truth. People spoke of tanks rolling closer, bridges being demolished, and soldiers vanishing overnight. Radios crackled with tense voices. Neighbors gathered in small clusters, murmuring about the Communists taking over.

I listened with more curiosity than fear. I wondered what the Communists looked like. In my childish imagination, they seemed almost unreal, like ghosts from stories. But when they finally arrived, they looked like ordinary men. Their uniforms were different, yet they were not monsters. Still, their presence changed everything.

The bridges around Bình Tuy were destroyed before the tanks could reach us. Fighting never directly reached our streets, but fear did. We knew my father's connection to the military placed our family in grave danger — a mark that could not be erased.

◆

During that first month, my parents made a swift decision. We packed what we could and moved to Vũng Tàu — nearly a hundred kilometers south along the coast — hoping American ships were still waiting to evacuate those who could flee.

It was the first time I realized that home could disappear overnight, and that we might never return to the life we once knew.

We stayed in a large empty house for three weeks, staring out at the sea every day, waiting.

No ships came.

Hope slowly twisted into fear.

We returned briefly to Bình Tuy, then sold our house and traveled north to Huế, where my grandparents lived — nearly a thousand kilometers up the length of Vietnam, a journey that in ordinary times would have taken days.

The long journey north felt like drifting between worlds — no longer belonging to the place we left, yet not fully rooted in the place ahead.

They welcomed us with open arms, grateful that we were still alive. Huế became a place to breathe and regroup, a temporary oasis amid the chaos. But even there, the future remained uncertain.

I went back to school and tried to focus on my lessons while my parents fought silently to rebuild some kind of normal life. In the middle of that year, my sister Hoa was born — a small, fierce cry that proved life was still moving forward.

◆

I cherished every stolen moment there, those fleeting glimpses of peace.

Night after night, my oldest brother and I crept along pitch-black paths, carrying tiny oil lamps to catch frogs for the family pot. By day, I volunteered for every grueling task. During planting season, we soaked seeds until they burst with green life, then bent our backs transplanting them into flooded fields under a scorching sun. At harvest, I carried towering bundles of rice on my thin shoulders. The rule was brutal: never set them down. The cut stalks hung downward, and if they touched the ground, the grains would loosen and fall away into the mud. Every drop meant less food. If your legs burned and your back screamed in agony, you could only shift the weight from one shoulder to the other.

One golden afternoon, fishing with older boys, I hooked an enormous fish. The thrill exploded in my chest — I had done something big, something that mattered.

Then, three months before we left, everything shattered. Grandfather fell ill with a sickness none of us understood. We watched him suffer and fade, helpless to do anything but stay beside him. He passed away not long after, leaving behind a silence in the house that no one knew how to fill.

Looking back, those village days — hard as they were — felt like the last pocket of peace in my childhood.

◆

But beneath the quiet surface, my parents carried a raging storm. My father could never return to his old job. My mother fought daily to feed nine mouths on almost nothing. Safety was a lie we told ourselves each night, masking the gnawing fear.

They saw the truth we children could not: love and shelter were no longer enough.

So, in the dead of night, we packed again and fled south to Đồng Tháp Mười — nine hundred kilometers back down the country we had just crossed — chasing one final desperate hope among the rivers and endless fields.

This time, the journey did not feel like a search for safety. It felt like a step deeper into the unknown — and the real hell was still ahead.

Chapter 2

THE GREAT FLOOD

After a year and a half in Huế, we packed our lives once more and moved south to Đồng Tháp Mười, hoping the land and rivers could keep us alive.

We claimed a small piece of farmland and built a fragile wooden boat with our own hands. River fishing was completely new to us. Every knot, every cast of the net, every pull against the current had to be learned through trial and bone-deep fear, our muscles aching under the relentless sun. Survival became our daily rhythm.

We planted rice, sweet potatoes — especially the rich purple ones whose taste still lingers in my memory — and rows of soursop and star gooseberry trees. For the first time since the war, we ate what the earth and water gave us. Life remained hard, but it finally felt like we were standing on solid ground.

In 1977, twin sisters arrived — Hiền and Hậu — born into that small piece of hard-won stability. Two new lives, two more reasons to keep going. Our family was now nine children, and our parents' shoulders carried more than ever. Yet somehow, the twins' arrival felt like a quiet signal that life was still moving forward, still insisting on itself despite everything.

◆

Until 1978.

The flood came like the wrath of God. Rain fell without mercy, pounding endlessly. Rivers rose quietly at first, then suddenly spilled over their banks. Water rushed into the fields, through the paths between homes, and finally into our house. Within days, the flood reached my chest as I stood inside. The floodwater carried a smell I have never forgotten — thick, dark, and alive with rot, like the earth itself was decomposing beneath us.

For nearly two weeks, our canoe became our lifeline. We paddled through what had once been streets and farmland, catching fish simply to survive. My mother cooked whatever we brought home, stretching every meal as far as possible, her face etched with worry.

Even small mistakes carried heavy consequences. One early morning, after eating too much sugar cane on an empty stomach, I developed severe stomach pain. The agony grew until my father and older brother had to stop working and carry me to the hospital in a small canoe. I thought I was going to die.

School never reopened for me after that. I left sixth grade forever. My older brother left eighth grade as well.

Childhood ended quietly.

There were no tears. Only work — heavy, and unending.

What haunted me most were the lightning storms. When thunder split the sky and lightning exploded overhead, I would crawl alone beneath the tiny hull of our boat, curled into a ball while the world shook violently. Each blinding flash made me certain this was the end. My brothers laughed and called me a coward.

"Coward!" one teased.

But I never told them how deeply that fear lived inside my bones.

◆

I was only twelve when I began walking to the market with my mother, sitting alone on the cold, muddy ground, the wet earth pressing through my thin clothes as I sold fish while she searched for anything we could eat. There was no tomorrow in my mind, only the next meal and the gnawing hunger that never fully left.

During those years, my parents began meeting friends who had relatives in America. At first, they were just familiar faces — neighbors, distant acquaintances, people who stopped by in the evenings after long days of work. They sat together on low wooden stools, sharing tea in the dim light of a small oil lamp, their voices casual, almost ordinary.

But slowly, something changed. Their conversations grew quieter, more guarded. When strangers passed by, the voices dropped even lower, sometimes stopping completely. I would watch from a corner, pretending not to listen, but I could feel the tension in the air.

They spoke of people who had made it out — families who had reached America after days at sea. They mentioned distant names, places I had never heard of, and whispered about boats, routes, and chances. Sometimes, a single word would linger in the air — escape — before being quickly swallowed by silence.

My father listened more than he spoke. His face remained still, but his eyes carried a weight I did not yet understand. My mother asked careful questions, her voice soft but steady, as if each answer mattered more than anything else.

Even as children, we knew not to ask. We did not understand the details, but we understood this: something was being planned. Something dangerous. Something that could change everything.

It felt like standing on a riverbank, watching the current pull faster than it should — knowing, without being told, that something ahead was about to break.

◆

At night, we secretly listened to the BBC with the volume turned low. We heard stories of Vietnamese refugee boats rescued at sea. Each story felt like a small light shining from far away.

"Listen," Father whispered one night. "Another boat was saved."

Those distant voices carried dreams into our small home.

Looking back, Đồng Tháp Mười was never just a place of survival. It was the secret birthplace of escape.

The flood of 1978 did not only drown our fields; it drowned every reason to stay, sweeping them all away.

The same rivers that had once kept us alive were now quietly calling us toward the open sea. But that sea — with its raging waves, lurking pirates, and no guarantee of survival — would it swallow us whole, or deliver us to freedom?

Chapter 3

WHERE THE DREAM TOOK ROOT

After the flood, life slipped back into its familiar rhythm, but something inside our family had quietly shifted forever, like a seed sprouting in the dark.

We worked harder than ever, yet we seemed to stand still. Each day repeated the same grueling cycle: rising before dawn, farming the land, fishing the rivers, collapsing into sleep long after dark. Food came in enough to survive, but the future felt narrower with every passing year. The communist regime rewarded neither hard work nor questions. It demanded only obedience and silence.

My parents saw it all too clearly, the worry written plainly on their faces.

They watched their children grow strong from endless labor, but they feared our minds were slowly starving, craving knowledge that was being choked off.

School had already ended for my older brother and me. For the younger ones, learning felt fragile and uncertain, always one step from vanishing. Teachers came and went often. Lessons remained shallow. Books were rare. Hope grew even scarcer.

At night, my parents spoke in low voices. They talked about education, faith, and the future they still dreamed of giving their children. They understood that under this regime, school was no longer a safe or fair path — especially for a family marked by a military past like ours. The past followed us no matter how far we tried to run.

They believed freedom was the true foundation of learning. Without freedom, knowledge had no space to breathe or grow; it became twisted and controlled.

◆

By the end of 1978, at fifteen and thirteen, my brother and I were still boys, but life refused to let us feel young. Our small frames carried the weight of grown men. We labored under the sun for eight hours or more, shifting between fields and water without pause, sweat stinging our eyes and backs screaming in pain.

We never complained. Work had become as natural as breathing.

Fishing gradually grew beyond mere survival. It turned into routine, duty, almost a second quiet profession alongside farming. Some days we took turns carrying fish to the market so our mother could sell them.

Those long walks remain gentle memories, though they were filled with fatigue. The market was never near, yet every step held purpose. Each fish we carried meant another meal secured, another day the family could hold on.

The plan that had first taken shape in Đồng Tháp Mười was now quietly gathering momentum, moving forward without words but with growing certainty.

At night we still tuned the radio to BBC, still listening for the same stories of boats that had made it out.

One evening, a man my father trusted came quietly to our house. I remember his face in the dim light, his voice barely above a whisper. He spoke of a cousin who had escaped by boat and reached a refugee camp.

"Not everyone makes it," he said softly. "But some do."

My father did not answer right away. He sat still, his hands resting on his knees, absorbing every word. My mother lowered her eyes, her fingers tightening around the edge of her scarf.

I did not understand everything they were discussing, but I understood the silence that followed. It was heavier than any words.

That night, nothing was decided out loud. But something inside our family had quietly crossed a line.

Every tale made the impossible feel slightly less impossible.

◆

In 1980, life slowed once more when our mother gave birth to our youngest brother, Út. A new baby brought fresh worries, fresh tenderness, and a deeper, quieter patience to the house.

The dream of escape never faded. It simply sank deeper into silence, waiting for the right moment.

We stayed in Đồng Tháp Mười until 1981. That year stands sharp in my memory because of the radio news. One night we heard President Ronald Reagan had been shot. Soon after, we learned Pope John Paul II had been shot as well. Two men from distant worlds, both surviving.

Even as a boy, I felt how fragile life could be, no matter where one lived. If men that powerful could be struck down and still survive, perhaps our family — small and invisible to the world — could survive too.

That same year, my parents traveled to scout a spot near Bà Rịa, closer to the sea. By the end of 1981, we moved fully to Phú Mỹ, near the village of Ngọc Hà — a place people whispered about for its steady stream of departures.

We arrived as strangers. We could not simply blend in. Father paid two ounces of gold to register us as permanent residents. That gold came from years of sweat, discipline, and sacrifice. Nothing was given freely.

Yet that payment quietly nudged our future forward.

◆

While waiting for the larger boat to be finished, we used a small rowboat fitted with portable sails. Those trips were never just for fishing. They became lessons, explorations, a slow familiarization with the open sea, its salty air biting our skin and restless waves testing our balance.

Fishing slowly stopped being only about survival. It became preparation. At first, I thought my parents were simply teaching us how to live. Only later did I realize they were teaching us how to leave.

In the evenings after work, we sometimes gathered around maps. My parents encouraged us to wonder about the world beyond Vietnam. A compass became more than a tool. It became a quiet promise of possibility and freedom.

In 1982, a new world opened. Ocean fishing was unlike anything we had known: the salt in the air, the sharper winds whipping our faces, and the endless waves crashing relentlessly. Each day the sea surprised us with new kinds of fish, vibrant and dangerous.

But this new life carried a silent goodbye. We could no longer keep farming. The land that once shaped our days slipped slowly from our grasp. Our lives now belonged entirely to the ocean. Everything depended on tides, winds, and patience.

Several days each month, we spent the night on the water. Those nights became some of my most cherished memories, though they were exhausting. We brought a small charcoal stove and cooked whatever the sea offered — fresh fish, and when luck smiled, crabs. I truly loved those nights. The smell of grilled fish drifting through the cool sea air, the gentle sway of the boat, the vast sky stretching endlessly above, sparkling with stars. Somehow food always tasted better out there. Maybe because of hunger. Maybe because of youth. Or maybe because of the simple, pure joy in those moments, whose real beauty only reveals itself years later.

Yet even in those quiet moments, we knew the danger was never far away. Surveillance, whispers, and sudden disappearances reminded us we were never truly unseen. Yet determination grew quietly inside our family.

By the end of 1982, that dream was no longer just a thought passed between hushed voices. It had become direction. Nothing was said aloud. Nothing was written. Trust was thin and carefully protected. The same waters that had taught us survival would soon carry us toward the unknown. But would it lead us to freedom?

Chapter 4

THE FIRST TO GO

Toward the end of 1982, my parents met old friends whose escape plan had already been carefully prepared. Everything was quietly arranged, and their departure was set for March 1983. For years, escape had lived only in whispers and careful glances. Now, suddenly, it had a date.

For our family, this was not just another conversation. It was the first real opportunity after years of waiting.

My parents had hoped to send two children, but plans, no matter how careful, can change in a moment. When the final hour arrived, the boat had no space left. In the end, only my third brother, Ánh, received the first ticket out of Vietnam toward America. It was a pain only parents can understand — to place their child into the hands of the sea and fate.

That single decision changed everything for us.

The first escape in our family did not begin with me. It began with Ánh.

In 1983, Ánh was only fifteen. My parents made the most painful choice of their lives. They sent him first and placed him in the hands of my father's friends. They believed that if even one child reached freedom, hope would stay alive for the rest of us.

Letting him go was an act of pure faith, laced with suppressed tears and silent prayers.

◆

That year, a fishing boat carrying forty-four people slipped quietly away from Vietnam, heading toward Indonesia. The boat carried more dreams than supplies. Food, fuel, and drinking water were dangerously low. Every mile brought a new question of life or death.

After four days at sea, the engine died when the boat ran out of fuel. The boat drifted helplessly for more than a full day. The sun beat down without mercy, burning skin raw. Thirst clawed at every throat. Fear spread through the crowded hull. No one knew where the currents were taking them or whether they would live to see land again.

Then a Thai fishing boat appeared on the horizon. The fishermen did not rescue them right away. But they offered something just as vital. They traded gold for fuel, rice, and water. With that small miracle, the boat could continue.

Several more days passed before they reached land. After seven days at sea, the boat arrived near Kuku Island in Indonesian waters. Local villagers helped guide them to safety. From there, they were taken to another island for paperwork. Finally, Red Cross workers brought them to Galang Island, the largest refugee camp in Indonesia.

◆

For Ánh, the dangers of the ocean were only the beginning.

Because he was a minor, he qualified for a special program. He told them he had relatives in the United States — he had been in contact with distant family connections, though no confirmed address could be provided at first.

After months of waiting that felt like years, he was accepted for resettlement.

Ánh spent eight long months in the refugee camp. He ate most meals alone, surrounded by languages he did not yet speak, counting days on a small calendar he kept folded in his pocket.

He did not know who his sponsors would be or where he would live. He asked no questions. He simply waited and accepted what came next, loneliness gnawing at him every night.

When Ánh finally stepped onto American soil in New York that December, he was wearing thin sandals. No one had warned him that winter in America could cut straight to the bone.

He did not complain. He only felt the freezing strangeness of everything around him. His sponsor's parents saw it immediately and handed him warm socks. Such a small gesture melted a little of his loneliness in that vast new world.

◆

Looking back, his escape was unbelievably fortunate. The boat met no pirates. No violent storms struck. The engine never failed again after the trade. There was no dramatic rescue, only quiet endurance sustained by chance meetings and sudden mercy from above.

By the grace of God, everyone on that boat reached safety.

Ánh's journey became the proof our family desperately needed.

It proved to my parents that escape was possible. It gave them courage to keep planning. And it planted a hope that refused to die — that one day we would all stand together in freedom.

But Ánh's escape was only the beginning. Ahead lay storms, imprisonment, and the agony of separation. Would our family find each other again — or shatter forever into the vast unknown?

1983, Brother Ánh on the left, Galang, refugee camp in Indonesia

Chapter 5

PREPARING TO LEAVE

After my fifteen-year-old brother Ánh escaped in 1983, no one in town knew. But inside our home, everything felt different, charged with a dangerous mix of hope and dread.

If one child could reach freedom, perhaps the rest of us could too. Yet every successful escape made the authorities more suspicious. Everyone knew families were trying to flee. Everyone knew boats were leaving at night, and not all of them survived.

Fishing had already become our way of life. My oldest brother Thành and I worked on the rivers full-time. We learned about the water, the tides, and the weather. We learned how to endure heat that scorched our skin, cold that numbed our fingers, hunger that clawed at our stomachs, and exhaustion that blurred our vision.

What had begun as quiet preparation in Đồng Tháp Mười had now become something far more urgent — a race against time and suspicion.

My parents understood that if we wanted any chance to escape by sea, we needed skills that could not be learned in a classroom. We needed to understand engines, fuel, navigation, and how to stay calm when everything went wrong — when waves crashed over the bow and death felt only a breath away.

We heard stories of boats that escaped successfully, and stories of boats that were shot at, boats that sank, families that disappeared forever. The sea was not only a path to freedom. It was also a graveyard.

Still, my parents refused to let go of the dream. They spoke quietly at home and planned in silence. They trusted no one. Under that system, words were dangerous, and even a small mistake could bring disaster.

◆

Eventually our daily fishing trips moved farther south, closer to the sea near Vũng Tàu, so we could learn ocean fishing and escape routes. River fishing was no longer enough. Ocean waves were different, higher, fiercer, unforgiving. The tides were stronger. The wind could change everything in minutes. If we were going to leave, we had to understand the sea.

Our family hired professionals to renovate our small river boat into a slightly larger one with a one-liter engine producing sixty to eighty horsepower. The structure had to be reshaped properly to handle ocean waves, which were far more violent than river currents.

Even while we prepared, we knew we were being watched. Police and local officials paid close attention to fishermen. They monitored those who traveled, who bought extra fuel, who repaired boats, and who spoke to strangers. In those days, even owning a decent boat could attract suspicion.

At one point, the authorities took my father, my brother Thành, and me to a local jail for interrogation. They questioned us about escape plans. They beat my father and my older brother. They did not beat me, but I was terrified.

I realized then that they did not need proof to punish someone. Suspicion alone could bring violence.

After that, our planning became even quieter. Despite the beating, despite the fear, we did not stop. We could not afford to.

◆

After my brother Ánh escaped, my parents arranged for me to try another escape. We paid the fare, and I was taken with five others to a small island near Bà Rịa.

Each day, someone brought us two handfuls of rice and a small piece of fish. We slept on the bare ground. We had no shoes. Sharp thorns pierced our heels with every step. Three days and three nights passed in hunger, thirst, and growing fear.

There was no water. We had to take it from the river below and drink it raw, risking sickness with every foul sip. At night we hid behind thick bushes so no one could see us. Sleep came in fits, interrupted by constant worry and the worst torment: mosquitoes. The swarm was relentless, driving us to the edge of madness. We dared not bring blankets or extra clothes, for fear of raising suspicion that we were preparing to flee.

Every night, when a ship passed by and shone its lights our way, terror surged through us. We froze, hearts pounding, afraid they suspected us of escaping and would send men to capture us.

Finally, we realized we had been deceived. There was no boat coming.

We decided to return to shore. We waded across a shallow river and walked along the rice fields for nearly a kilometer until we reached the highway. Every step was agony, our feet bleeding from thorns. We moved in silence, hearts racing, terrified of encountering farmers working the fields. If anyone saw a group of strangers, ragged and suspicious, they might report us, and the authorities would come.

I had no money left. When I climbed onto a bus, I noticed a woman about the same age as my mother. I gathered my courage and told her I had been cheated. She looked at me with compassion and paid my fare. About thirty minutes later, I got off the bus near my home.

My mother cried with joy when she saw me return safely.

In those three days and three nights on the island, I lived in constant terror. I feared the authorities would discover us and throw me in prison. If that happened, all our careful planning would collapse.

That failed attempt did not stop us. It only strengthened our resolve.

It would become action. But when that moment arrived, would we slip through undetected — or be dragged back into interrogation rooms we might never leave?

Chapter 6

LEARNING THE COMPASS AND THE MAP

One night, long after the house had fallen silent, my brother spread a worn map across the wooden floor and placed a small compass at its center. The lantern flickered beside us, casting unsteady light over the thin paper.

None of us spoke.

We simply stared at it, understanding for the first time that freedom had a direction.

Fishing had taught us how to survive on the water, but survival alone was not enough. If we were going to leave Vietnam by sea, we needed more than strength — we needed certainty. Once land disappeared, there would be no second chances, only the vast ocean and whatever fate awaited us there.

That was when the compass and the map entered our lives.

At first, they felt unfamiliar in our hands, almost too simple for something that carried such weight. The compass did not argue or guess. It simply pointed north, steady and patient, like a quiet truth we could not ignore.

My brothers and I learned to trust it — by daylight and in the dim glow of a lantern at night — tracing lines across the map, measuring distance, imagining paths we had never seen.

Sometimes my brother would slide his finger slowly along the coastline, then out into open water.

"Here," he whispered once. "If we go this way, maybe we can reach there."

No one answered.

We studied quietly, long after the rest of the house had gone to sleep. We learned the names of nearby countries and the distances between them. We learned how currents could pull a boat away from its path, how wind could shift direction without warning, and how the shortest route was not always the safest.

Some paths led to freedom.

Others led nowhere.

◆

Around that same time, we learned another lesson — one that would matter just as much as direction.

The small engines we used for fishing often failed when salt water seeped inside. One day, before the mechanic arrived, my older brother and I decided to examine the engine ourselves. Piece by piece, we took it apart, laying each part carefully beside us. We cleaned what we could, studied how it fit together, and slowly rebuilt it.

When the mechanic finally arrived, he was furious.

He scolded us for touching something we did not understand.

But when the engine roared to life, everything changed.

That moment stayed with us. It taught us that knowledge did not always come from instruction — it could come from patience, observation, and the courage to try. It also showed us that when something failed, panic was not the only response. Calm thinking could bring it back to life.

One day, that lesson would stand between life and death.

◆

As our preparation deepened, the plan itself became more careful, more dangerous.

Our family knew that staying together would draw attention. Too many people moving at once would raise suspicion. If we were discovered, the consequences would be severe — financial loss, imprisonment, even torture.

So the decision formed slowly, through prayer and quiet discussion.

We would divide into smaller groups.

Each group would leave at a different time.

Supplies, fuel, and food were arranged in silence, stored separately so nothing appeared unusual. Every movement had to look ordinary, like daily life continuing without change.

Goodbyes were never spoken aloud.

We learned to say them without words.

Even with all the planning, fear never left us. It lingered in every glance, every quiet pause, every unspoken thought. But something else was growing alongside it — something steadier.

Direction.

Faith.

By then, the plan was no longer just a dream passed between hushed voices. It had taken shape, quiet but real, waiting for its moment.

The compass always pointed north.

Whether north meant freedom or death, we would not know until we were already at sea.

Chapter 7

MY ESCAPE – JUST A LITTLE TOUR

One day before our escape, my father submitted an official request to take the boat out for an engine test. A few hours later, it was approved. We now had permission to "test the engine" at sea.

That approval felt like a miracle. The very next morning we were leaving for good — and a simple official stamp had made it possible. If the request had been denied, the entire plan could have collapsed.

In Vietnam at that time, permission was not always about papers. Sometimes it was a bowl of hot phở, a pack of 555 cigarettes, and no more questions asked.

◆

The morning of our escape arrived quietly, just like any other fishing day.

Behind our small house was a narrow, hidden river. I had docked the boat there the night before so no one would notice. The river flowed about two kilometers before joining the Thị Vải River, where the water widened and opened the way to the sea.

Thirty minutes before departure, my oldest brother Thành slipped out of the house without a sound. He took a small rowing boat with one handicapped passenger. To anyone watching, it looked completely ordinary. Fishermen left early every morning. No one would suspect a thing.

I stayed behind, my heart pounding, watching and waiting.

At exactly eight o'clock, I stepped onto our boat. It looked harmless. A fishing net lay openly on deck. We carried only a small can of gasoline, just enough for what appeared to be a short trip.

Not far away, two large patrol boats sat docked, their powerful engines and mounted machine guns clearly visible.

For ten long minutes I stood frozen. Should I go first, or wait for them to leave? My hands were ice-cold even though the air was warm. My mind raced through every possible disaster. If I waited too long, suspicion might grow. If I left too soon, they might stop me.

I closed my eyes and prayed. I asked Mother Mary to protect me, to guide us, to hold us in her hands as we stepped into the unknown. I knew we were placing our lives completely in God's mercy.

Then I made the decision. I started the engine and slowly steered the boat out of the narrow river behind our house. The motor purred low and steadily.

I kept the speed normal, exactly like any ordinary fishing trip.

When I looked back, no one was following.

◆

Just before we reached the Thị Vải River, my younger brother Huy suddenly spoke.

"Brother, can we turn back?"

"I forgot my crickets."

His words cut straight into my heart. Tears rushed to my eyes, but I forced my voice to stay calm.

"We're only going out for a little tour," I told him. "We'll come back and get your crickets later."

But I knew the truth.

This was not a tour.

I turned my head for one last look at our town, our riverbanks, the familiar trees and houses I had known all my life. Everything I loved was right there behind me, fading away.

That was the last time I ever saw Vietnam.

I faced forward again, gripped the wheel, and let the current carry us toward the open sea.

◆

A little farther along, I spotted brother Thành's small rowing boat ahead. I approached quietly and picked him up along with the handicapped passenger. Everything still looked perfectly normal. That was exactly what we needed.

From there we continued to the meeting point. The second group was already waiting with extra fuel, food, supplies, and the rest of our passengers. My twelve-year-old brother Hoàng — quiet and careful beyond his years — had done his part the night before. He brought the precious compass and joined the second group.

Once everyone was safely aboard, we moved back into the Thị Vải River and headed straight for the place where the river meets the ocean, the river mouth near Vũng Tàu. We passed several large ships along the way. No one suspected anything. We looked like ordinary fishermen heading out for the day.

Only four of us stayed visible on deck: my brother and I, plus two others sitting in the cabin like normal crew. Everyone else stayed hidden beneath the floorboards, silent and motionless, breathing shallowly.

◆

When we reached the river mouth, the tide was low. River water rushed out to meet the sea while strong ocean winds pushed back. Waves slammed against the cabin roof, spraying water over us until we were completely soaked and chilled to the bone.

That was the most terrifying moment of my entire life. I had never passed this point before in all my years of fishing. Everything felt strange, dangerous, and unstoppable, with the roar of waves echoing in my ears.

But no one complained.

No one moved.

No one made a sound.

We simply held on — soaked, silent, and praying — our hearts clenching.

Somewhere behind us, a boy's crickets sat waiting in a house we would never see again. Somewhere ahead, the open sea held answers we were not yet brave enough to imagine.

Chapter 8

THE FIRST NIGHT IN THE OCEAN

We carried only one compass. Some people brought small pieces of gold or jewelry, the last fragments of the lives they hoped to rebuild somewhere far away. There were thirty-nine souls on our tiny boat.

When the engine finally started, a low rumble spread through the wooden hull. For a moment, no one spoke. The boat slowly pulled away from the dark shoreline, and every pair of eyes turned back toward land. Some people whispered quiet prayers. Others simply stared in silence, as if trying to memorize the last outline of the country we were leaving behind.

No one knew what waited for us ahead. All we knew was that the shore was fading, and with every meter the boat moved forward, the path behind us was closing forever.

◆

That first night on the open ocean, I discovered what darkness truly means. No land. No lights. Nothing but black water stretching in every direction.

The sea was not silent. Waves crashed and hissed against the wooden hull, the sound echoing through the night like the breathing of something enormous and alive.

Salt spray whipped across my face, stinging my eyes and burning my throat. Waves rose like angry walls, lifting the boat high into the air before slamming it back down with terrifying force. Each drop made my stomach lurch.

Many people were violently seasick. They groaned and vomited over the side. Some lay curled on the floor of the boat, too weak to even lift their heads. The smell inside the boat grew heavy and bitter — the sharp odor of gasoline mixed with saltwater and sickness. Every breath tasted of fuel and salt, and the rolling waves only made the sickness worse. Even the captain and the mechanic lay helpless, too sick to move.

◆

That left only my older brother and me.

We became real captains.

We became real mechanics.

Because we were the ones who had learned to tear an engine apart and put it back together with our own hands on the land. Now those same hands had to keep this boat alive in the middle of the sea, trembling with exhaustion and fear. Thirty-nine lives now depended on two young men who had never sailed the open ocean before.

The engine roared beneath our feet, and every strange sound made our hearts tighten. We checked the fuel, listened to the motor, and watched the compass again and again, afraid that one small mistake could send us drifting off course forever.

No matter how doubtful the eyes watching us were, we never stopped. We worked through the night, soaked and exhausted but determined, our fingers numb from the cold spray and the constant rolling of the boat. There was no time to think too much. If we let fear take over, the sea would defeat us before dawn.

◆

By six o'clock that evening — six hours after passing through the river mouth — we had traveled about eighty kilometers from shore.

I turned and looked back one last time. The coast had become nothing more than a faint smudge on the horizon.

For a brief moment, a thought about my family crossed my mind. I wondered whether my parents and my younger siblings were safe back home, or if the police would come asking questions after discovering that I had disappeared. The distance between us was growing with every wave, and there was nothing I could do for them now but keep moving forward.

For the first time that day, I let out a long, shaky breath.

No one was chasing us.

No one was stopping us.

We had made it this far.

We had escaped the land, but we had not yet understood what it meant to belong to the sea.

◆

The wind softened for a while, and the engine hummed steadily beneath our feet. I looked up at the sky. Thousands of stars burned above us, brighter than I had ever seen in my life.

The sea grew strangely quiet, as if the ocean itself was holding its breath. Beneath that endless sky, our small wooden boat felt like a single leaf drifting on a vast black ocean.

I had known rivers all my life. I knew flooded fields, canals, and the familiar waters of home. But this was different. This water had no edge, no mercy, and no promise. It did not care who we were or what dreams we carried.

Deep inside, fear whispered. The ocean was only beginning to show its teeth.

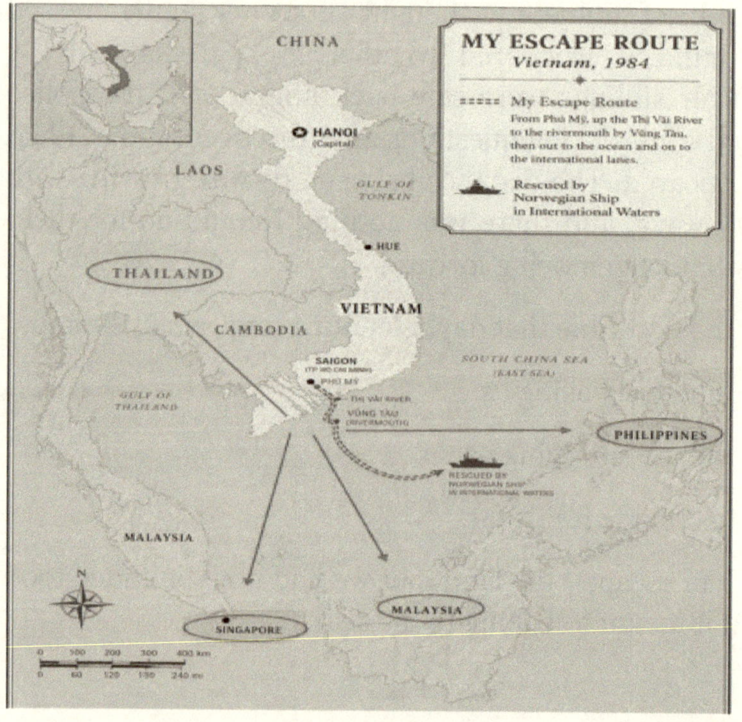

Thailand, the Philippines, Malaysia, and Singapore were places that hosted refugee camps providing food, clothing, shelter, and sponsorship for refugees. These efforts were supported by the U.S. government, the United Nations, churches, volunteer agencies, local community organizations, UNICEF, and other non-governmental organizations.

Chapter 9

THE ENGINE DIED AT 1 PM

On the second day, the waves still hammered the boat without mercy. The small fishing boat climbed one wall of water after another, then slammed hard into the troughs between them. Everyone looked utterly spent, their faces pale and hollow, as the merciless rocking battered them and salt crusted on their lips. The boat was heavy with too many people and too much fear. The engine labored louder than it should have, straining under the load, its rumble growing unsteady and ragged. It had been running since dawn, but by early afternoon I began to hear that something was wrong.

Then I heard it.

A cough. A sputter. The steady roar of the motor became uneven, like a man struggling to breathe.

Then it stopped.

The silence was terrifying.

The ocean did not care that our engine had stopped. The current kept pushing us, the wind kept rising, and our boat began drifting sideways in the water. We had only basic tools on board.

I looked at my brother. My voice was slow but steady:

"Let me open the fuel filter and clear the dust."

◆

My hands were already shaking as I crouched beside the engine. Saltwater sprayed across the deck while the boat rocked violently under my knees. I twisted the round filter. In that second a small stainless-steel piece, part of the spray nozzle, slipped free. It hit the deck with a tiny metallic sound.

Then it began to roll across the wet deck.

My heart stopped. Thirty-nine lives suddenly depended on a piece of metal no bigger than a fingernail.

The boat rocked.

The metal piece rolled.

That tiny metal bit tumbled like it had a life of its own, dodging my hands, slipping farther with each jolt. I lunged, missed, lunged again. Another wave struck the hull.

The boat tilted sharply, and the tiny metal piece spun farther away.

That was the moment panic exploded. I cried out loud, raw and helpless. I prayed with everything I had — not polite words, but desperate, soul-deep cries. I dropped to my knees and searched the wet floor again, knowing that if we lost that piece, we lost everything.

◆

In that moment, a terrible thought rushed through my mind. If the engine stayed dead and we could not fix it, the currents would slowly push our boat into the Gulf of Thailand. That place meant only death. Pirates roamed those waters. The women and girls on our boat could be taken away, and the rest of us beaten or even shot.

My brother and I were terrified. We had heard too many stories before leaving Vietnam — boats drifting helplessly into the Gulf of Thailand, passengers attacked, families disappearing without a trace.

As we kept searching for the missing piece and trying to repair the engine, we prayed at the same time, begging God not to let that fate become ours.

◆

Ten minutes stretched into forever.

Then I found it — glinting faintly in a crack between the boards. For a moment I could not breathe. I reached in carefully with trembling fingers and pulled it out.

My brother and I fought to fit it back into place. The boat lurched, our hands shook, salt burned our eyes, and the engine scalded our fingers. Every wave tried to throw us off, the sea roaring its challenge.

But we didn't stop.

For an hour and a half, we battled the sea and the machine, drawing on every memory of the day we tore an engine apart on dry land — even when the mechanic had yelled at us for daring to touch it.

Every few seconds another wave slammed into the hull. And each time I feared the engine would refuse to start. Finally, the engine coughed.

Once.

Then it roared back to life.

In that instant I felt something I'll carry forever: The sea had just let us live another day.

Someone cheered. Someone shouted:

"Thank the Lord!"

◆

Salt still stung our faces. Fear still gripped our chests. But hope — small, stubborn hope — came back to the boat.

A running engine meant the difference between drifting helplessly — or steering toward freedom. We understood that now in a way no words could have taught us.

Chapter 10

THE SHIP THAT TURNED BACK

After the engine roared back to life, something shifted on the boat. The gray exhaustion on every face softened just slightly. For the first time in days, people allowed themselves a small, careful hope.

When I left home that morning pretending to go fishing, I could not bring anything extra, not even a change of clothes. Anything more would have looked suspicious. So, I wore the same single set I always wore on the water. Now that shirt and those pants were soaked through with seawater and engine oil. Salt and grease clung to my skin. My hands smelled of diesel and metal. I was bone tired but alive, my body aching yet pulsing with relief.

After the engine came back to life, we set our course for Malaysia, trusting the compass and the map. Faces that had been gray with fear suddenly lit up. People smiled again. Hope filled the little boat. My brother and I were the happiest of all, because only we knew how close we had come to dying.

If that engine had stayed silent, none of this would have happened.

◆

That afternoon the sea grew calmer and we entered international waters. As darkness fell, the lights of great ships appeared on the horizon, blazing like floating cities on the water.

Every time those lights appeared, our hearts leaped.

Is that land?

Is that an island?

Are we finally safe?

But as we drew closer, the lights always drifted away. One ship after another passed us in the dark and kept going.

We counted them.

Eighty-one ships over three nights.

Hope would rise, then fall away again with every passing ship. Exhaustion carved deep lines into every face. Children stopped talking. Adults prayed in whispers. We rationed every drop of water and every bite of food. Still, we pushed forward, guided only by faith, the compass, and the stubborn will to live.

◆

Then, around eight o'clock on the third night after the sun had set, the sea turned against us. The wind rose suddenly, sharp and cold, cutting across the deck without mercy. It howled without stopping, carrying the briny smell of salt and the raw scent of fear.

An AI artist's reimagining of the third night, when the ocean turned violent.

Dark clouds rolled in, blotting out the stars. The waves grew taller and angrier, slamming into the boat with bone-jarring force. In the pitch-black night, we could hardly see the horizon and could no longer tell which way was forward. Every swell lifted us high, then dropped us into a deep trough. The hull groaned as if it might split apart. One wrong turn, one moment of lost direction, and the boat would capsize, thirty-nine lives swallowed by the sea.

Panic spread through the hull. People clutched one another. Children whimpered. Adults whispered frantic prayers. No one dared raise their voice above the roar of the wind and waves.

My brother Thành and I gripped the wheel together, our hands numb and our eyes fixed on the horizon we could barely see. We were terrified, but we said nothing. We only prayed silently, begging God to guide us through the night.

This was the third night I had not slept. Fear kept my eyes open and my mind racing. Every crash of a wave felt like the end.

◆

Around eight thirty, just when the storm seemed ready to break, something changed. The wind shifted suddenly and gently. The clouds parted just enough to let faint starlight through. The waves began to ease, no longer towering, no longer crashing with murderous force. The sea grew calmer, almost merciful. It was as if God Himself had heard our silent pleas.

I let out a long trembling breath, the first real breath in hours. Exhaustion crashed over me like a wave of its own.

I slumped against the side of the boat and, for the first time in three nights, allowed myself to close my eyes.

I slept for about an hour, but it was the deepest, most grateful sleep I had known since we left Vietnam.

While I rested, my brother Thành stayed at the wheel, steering through the quiet night, his face lit faintly by the compass light. He kept us on course, alone with the sea and with faith.

The storm had passed.

◆

Then everything changed.

That morning felt different. After so many ships had passed us by, I no longer expected anyone to stop. Each time we had steered toward a ship, hope rose in our hearts only to watch the lights drift away again.

But this time the sea was calm. Dawn was breaking. The sky was beautiful, painted with soft colors as the first light touched the water. The ocean lay quiet around us, almost peaceful, as if the storm of the night before had never existed.

Then we saw a ship in the distance. At first, it looked like all the others, just another shape on the horizon. But as the sun slowly rose, something unexpected happened.

The ship turned.

For a moment I thought my tired eyes were playing tricks on me.

It was heading toward us.

My heart began to race. After so many disappointments, I did not feel despair this time. I felt something else, a quiet, trembling hope.

Please don't go away from me. I saw you last night, and you sailed away. I cannot lose you again.

An AI artist reimagining the rescued ship was spotted in a distance

The ship was not sailing away. It had turned and was facing directly toward us.

We pushed the engine harder and steered our small boat toward the ship, because it seemed to be waiting for us.

When we were still about a quarter of a kilometer away, I saw tiny figures moving along the rail. Then came the moment I will remember until I die. A long rope ladder slowly dropped down the side of the ship. Crew members waved their hands to guide us.

For a moment no one moved. After drifting between life and death for three days, we were almost afraid to believe the rescue was real. Then one man from our boat stepped forward and grabbed the rope ladder. For a moment his hands slipped on the wet rope. Our bodies were so weak that even climbing that ladder felt like climbing a mountain.

Joy exploded across our boat. Faces that had been frozen in fear broke into tears and laughter. Some people cried out loud. Some fell to their knees and prayed. Children stared upward as if they were watching a miracle.

My brother Thành and I quickly organized the boarding, positioning ourselves at the foot of the ladder to keep order and steady the rope. The adults near the front climbed first. Then came the children — one small face looked up at the ladder, hesitated for just a moment, then reached up with both hands and climbed. The women followed, their trembling fingers gripping each rung as the rope swung with the motion of the waves. Finally, the remaining adults went up one by one.

The ladder swung constantly as our small boat rose and fell beneath it. People had to grip with everything they had just to keep their balance. My brother and I held the base steady, bracing against the hull, making sure no one lost their footing. We did not move until every single person was safely aboard.

An AI artist's reimagining Rope ladder from the Norwegian ship

Only after we carefully counted every person and made sure no one had been left behind did my brother and I finally leave our little boat.

When I grasped the ladder with both hands, I already felt the joy of being rescued. I knew we were going to live.

◆

Once everyone climbed onto the ship's deck, most of the others quickly went inside the cabin, overwhelmed with happiness. But I turned toward the ocean. Our small fishing boat was drifting away. For a moment, I simply stood there and watched.

The engine was silent now. The waves rocked the boat gently as it moved farther and farther from the ship. That little wooden boat had carried thirty-nine lives across the open sea. I had repaired its engine with my own hands, steered it through storm and fear, and trusted it when nothing else was certain.

My eyes filled with tears as I looked back at the small boat, grateful for that humble companion that had carried us through the last few days.

That last glance was my quiet goodbye.

For three days, that boat had been our only piece of land in the middle of the ocean.

After wiping the tears from my eyes, I looked up and saw the Norwegian crew welcoming us with warm smiles and gentle kindness. For a few moments, happiness overwhelmed me. Then I walked back to the ship's rail and waved one last goodbye to my old wooden friend. The boat drifted slowly away, smaller and smaller, until it disappeared into the wide ocean.

Sometimes freedom begins with a farewell.

◆

We had brought a framed picture of Saint Martin with us for courage, but in the shock and joy of rescue we forgot to take it. Even now I still feel the loss of that picture, a gentle sadness in my chest.

And then came one more moment I will never forget. As we turned toward the big ship, dolphins suddenly appeared. They swam beside us, in front of us, and behind us, moving with our boat like an escort. They stayed with us at the exact moment we changed direction.

For the first time in days, people on our boat began to smile again.

I do not know why they came. But I know what I felt. It was as if God Himself had sent them to guide us home.

The ship was the **Essy Silje**.

It was the **eighty-first** ship.

The ship that turned back to rescue us.

◆

The crew treated us with a kindness that still moves me today. They cut their own white work uniforms to fit our small bodies. The clothes looked strange, almost funny. But every stitch was made with mercy.

They gave us food. Beef links. Hot dogs. Bread. Milk. Milk was new to most of us. Some people had stomach pain, but no one complained. After everything we had survived, a little pain felt like nothing.

No one needed medicine. What we needed most was compassion, and the crew gave it freely.

Only one or two of us could speak English. We did not understand their words, but we understood their eyes and their hands.

They told us they would take us to Singapore and then to a refugee camp. The journey would take one more day. That night they showed us movies. For a few hours, we were just people watching a screen, and that was enough.

We were safe.

◆

As the big ship moved forward again, this time carrying us, I stood quietly on the deck and looked out at the endless ocean. I thought of my parents. I thought of my little brothers and sisters still in Vietnam. I thought of the prayer I whispered just before I started the engine that morning.

Life and death had balanced on the tip of my fingers.

By God's grace, life had won.

But even as relief flooded through me, a quiet voice inside whispered: This is not the end. The sea had let us go, but the real journey was only beginning.

Looking back now, I realize something I did not understand then. Sometimes hope does not come when we expect it. It comes after we have already lost the strength to hope.

Chapter 11

SINGAPORE – THE FIRST SAFE GROUND

Before we left the ship, we said goodbye to the Norwegian crew of the Essy Silje. We did not share the same language, but their kindness needed no translation. They had pulled thirty-nine strangers from the edge of death and treated us like family.

When my feet finally touched land in Singapore, it felt like stepping into another world.

For the first time since we left Vietnam, everything was calm. No rushing waves. No roaring engines. No fear chasing us from behind. We were safe, and we knew it deep in our bones. The United Nations was helping us now and just knowing that lifted a mountain of weight from my chest. I could finally breathe freely, the air clean and steady.

Singapore was the cleanest, most beautiful country I had ever seen. There was no trash on the streets, no dirt on the buses, no chaos anywhere. Everything looked perfectly organized, modern, and respected. After days of salt, oil, and terror on the ocean, the simple sight of clean sidewalks made something inside me stir. For the first time in years, I dared to believe that life could one day feel normal again.

◆

At the refugee camp, my body finally began to relax. The constant fear that had lived in my blood since the open sea slowly loosened its grip. They told us we would stay in Singapore for three months before being moved to Bataan Refugee Camp in the Philippines to wait for a country to accept us.

At that moment we did not know where our future would lead. We only knew one thing for certain: we were still alive.

Later we learned that Norway had been willing to accept us. But there was only one place on earth where we needed to go. Ánh was already there — fifteen years old when he escaped, now living under foster care in America, waiting for the family he had left behind. The United States understood this. They accepted us not as strangers, but as a family that needed to be whole again.

For the first time in my life, the word "future" felt real.

◆

Life in Singapore slowly found a gentle rhythm again. We attended English classes nearly every day, a few hours each morning. Other refugees studied French, Swedish, or Norwegian depending on where they hoped to go. I felt secretly thankful that English came more naturally to us. It felt like a door slowly opening instead of a wall blocking our way.

We were allowed to live like human beings once more.

We could attend church. Once a week we were allowed to explore downtown, where people ate out in places that reminded me of Chinatown.

What I wanted most was to step inside a movie theater. Where I grew up in Vietnam, I had never had the chance to watch a film on the big screen.

We had regular meals and even a little money for bus rides. After so many years of survival, these small things felt like miracles — warm food in our stomachs, clean beds at night, and the quiet safety of routine.

◆

Yet every night when the lights went out, the same heavy thoughts returned. I lay awake thinking about my parents, and my younger brothers and sisters still trapped in Vietnam. Had they escaped? Were they safe? The joy of being alive was always mixed with a faint ache of memory, a longing for them that gnawed at my heart and kept sleep away.

One of the greatest blessings in Singapore was our English teacher, Elizabeth, an Indian woman whose kindness went far beyond her job. She took us to her home on the 35th floor, the first time I had ever ridden an elevator that high. She cooked dinner for us and let us watch science fiction movies together like we were family. Those simple evenings touched me deeply. They reminded me that not every stranger in this world was dangerous — some were angels in disguise.

Singapore itself looked like a dream. The city sparkled — clean, bright, and modern. In my eyes, it felt like heaven compared to everything we had run from. I often stood quietly and thought to myself: if the world could be this beautiful, perhaps my own future could be bright as well.

◆

But the three months passed faster than we expected. Then one day, we were placed on an airplane and flown to the Bataan Refugee Camp in the Philippines.

Singapore had been our first safe ground. Bataan would be an entirely different chapter.

Singapore had given us something we had almost forgotten how to feel — the quiet, ordinary joy of being alive without fear. We carried that feeling forward like a gift we intended to keep.

Chapter 12

BATAAN, PHILIPPINES: THE WAITING ISLAND

When I first set foot in Bataan, I felt both grateful and heartbroken at the same time. I was grateful because we were finally safe. But I was heartbroken because Bataan was still not our destination.

This was a large refugee camp on an island, a few hours' drive from Manila. We were so close to the real world that we could see Manila's city lights sparkling at night, yet iron fences and strict rules still held us apart from it — freedom visible but just out of reach.

The camp was filled with thousands of people from many different countries. Everyone carried their own pain, their own story, and their own stubborn hope. We slept with two or three people in a room. It was not comfortable, but it was enough for the time being. Every day we were given rice, fish, pork, and chicken. After the hunger and terror on the ocean, simply having enough to eat felt like an enormous blessing, nourishing our battered bodies and quieting the constant ache in our stomachs.

Life slowly found its rhythm again. We attended English classes five days a week. Every Sunday a bus took us to church. Church was where I found real peace. Sitting there, listening to the hymns rise in the humid air, I felt clearly that I was still a human being, still loved by God, and still moving forward even while waiting. The words of prayer wrapped around me like a blanket, soothing the raw edges of my heart.

◆

But the strongest emotion in Bataan was no longer fear — it was a deep, aching boredom and homesickness that settled into our bones like the humid tropical air.

We missed home so much it hurt. We missed the sound of our little siblings laughing, the familiar smell of the river at dawn, even the old fears that had once kept us alert.

Every afternoon, when I looked out at the sea, I quietly asked myself: Where are my parents and my youngest brother and sisters now? Are they waiting to hear from us?

It was hard to explain how we felt, because we did not know how to send a letter or what words could possibly describe the journey we had survived. Still, we believed they had already received the telegram we sent three months earlier, letting them know that we had reached safety in Singapore.

The ache deepened with each passing day, a silent wound that never quite closed.

◆

After each day in ESL class, I tried to read a little, hoping to prepare myself for the future and for this new language. English words felt like climbing a mountain to me. I did not even have a strong foundation in my own Vietnamese because I had stopped going to school seven years earlier.

I would hold a small book and try to read, but I understood very little. At nineteen years old, my mind was still struggling at about a fifth-grade level. It was frustrating and discouraging.

I kept asking myself the same questions again and again:

"What am I going to do when I arrive in America? Will I just get a nine-to-five job, earn money, and send it back to Vietnam for my parents? Or should I try to go back to school? But who would accept someone like me into high school?"

I had no answers then. But the questions themselves told me something important — I was still dreaming, and that meant I was still alive inside.

These thoughts circled endlessly in my mind during my time in the Bataan camp. The future felt heavy and uncertain.

Sometimes at night, when the camp grew quiet, I would think of my parents still in Vietnam. They had risked everything so their children might have a chance at freedom. I knew that whatever future waited for me in America, I had to make it worth the sacrifice they had made.

◆

Yet amid the waiting and the longing, small moments of joy found their way in — like unexpected gifts from strangers who slowly became friends.

I made a few close friends in the camp, young people like me who carried the same quiet ache for home. In the evenings, when the heat of the day finally eased, we would gather in a quiet corner of the compound with an old, borrowed guitar. Someone would strum a few chords, and soon we were singing together, our voices blending into the warm tropical night.

For a little while, the music helped us forget the endless uncertainty and the faces we missed so dearly.

I learned two songs by heart just by listening and trying to follow along. One was Hotel California by the Eagles — its story of a traveler trapped in a beautiful but inescapable place felt strangely fitting for our own journey. The other was How Can I Tell Her by Lobo. I did not fully understand its words then, only its feeling — something tender and unspoken that lived quietly in the melody. I practiced it again and again on that borrowed guitar, not knowing that one day I would sing it from the heart in a circle of people I had not yet met, in a country I had not yet reached.

We sang them repeatedly, laughing when we got the words wrong, clapping when someone hit a high note just right.

Those simple melodies turned strangers into brothers, and for those brief hours, the camp felt less like a prison and more like a temporary home.

Those guitar nights were small gifts — reminders that even in waiting, life could still hold beauty, laughter, and connection.

◆

The hardest part was still waiting. Weeks turned into months. We filled out forms, stood in lines, answered the same questions again. Every medical checkup felt like a test we could not afford to fail. Every interview with resettlement officers carried the weight of our entire future. Hope held on, but doubt crept in — would America really take us? Would we be separated again? Would we ever be whole?

One day the final test came. It was the day of the full medical examination. My three brothers and I stood in line, hearts pounding. The doctors examined us very carefully: chest X-rays, blood tests, checking every centimeter. We were lucky. All four of us were healthy. The papers were signed. Our future opened.

But right after that, I watched my close friends break down in tears. Some had tuberculosis. Some had hepatitis. Some had old scars on their lungs that showed up on the X-ray. They had to stay behind.

I hugged them tightly, tears rolling down my face. We had crossed the ocean together, we had died and come back to life together, and now because of one small scar on a lung, they had to remain on this waiting island, their dreams delayed in agony.

◆

The four of us were told we would fly to America in a few weeks. After everything we had survived — the ocean, the storms, the waiting — those words felt almost too simple for what they meant. We packed what little we had, said goodbye to the friends we were leaving behind, and quietly prepared ourselves for the last leg of a journey that had begun so many years ago on a narrow river behind our house.

Chapter 13

AMERICA – THE FIRST MORNING OF A NEW LIFE

On the night of February 25, 1985, our plane descended through clouds and landed in New York City. After everything — the rivers, the ocean, the camps, the waiting — we had finally arrived. Winter was already more than halfway over, yet for me it still felt like stepping onto a completely different planet.

The next morning in the hotel I woke up with only one thought burning in my mind.

I want to see snow.

I had never seen snow in my life. I wanted to touch it, feel it, understand it with my own body. So I put on shorts and rode the elevator down with a few Americans.

When I reached the ground floor and walked toward the exit, a gentleman looked at me and asked gently,

"Aren't you cold?"

I did not know how to answer properly. My English was still very poor and I was nervous. The first words that came out of my mouth were,

"Never mind."

He smiled. I could tell he knew right away that I was brand new to this country and to this language. Later when I told my family what I had said, everyone laughed until they cried. But at that moment it was not funny at all. I felt small and embarrassed.

Still, I stepped outside.

The winter air hit me like a wall of ice. I stood there freezing, but completely amazed. I looked at the falling snow like a child staring at magic. Soft white flakes drifted down, landing on my bare arms, melting instantly against my skin. I reached out and caught one on my palm — it was so light, so perfect, gone in a second. I did not want to go back inside. I wanted to stay there forever, because this was the very first morning of my new life, filled with wonder and possibility.

◆

Later that morning I walked into the coffee shop next to the hotel. I stood in line to buy breakfast, but I had no idea how to order anything. My mind was spinning with fear.

What if they ask me questions?

What if I do not understand?

What if I embarrass myself again?

I pointed to the man in front of me and said,

"The same."

Inside my heart I was praying,

Please understand. Please do not ask me anything else.

Somehow it worked.

◆

I was still smiling from the coffee shop when, by noon that same day, everything changed once more. My brother Ánh arrived at the hotel with his foster parents. The moment I saw him I could not hold back my tears. I cried because I had missed him so much. I cried because he was alive. I cried because I never thought I would see him again so soon.

I was so happy, especially knowing he already had people who loved him and supported him in this new country.

At that moment, New York stopped feeling like a strange and frightening place. For the first time it began to feel like home might be possible again.

But deep inside, something kept whispering. We had finally reached America. We had stepped onto the land of our dreams. But dreams, we were learning, were only the beginning — the real work of becoming was just about to start.

Chapter 14

WALTON HIGH SCHOOL – BRONX, NEW YORK
(1985)

The real work of becoming began in the Bronx, in a small apartment, with nothing but a fresh start and everything to prove.

An agency called USCC helped us with our legal papers and assisted us in finding a small apartment in the Bronx.

Because my older brother and I were already over eighteen, we were allowed to live independently, just the two of us in the Bronx. But my two younger brothers Hoàng and Huy were placed with foster parents upstate. We had survived the ocean together, yet America separated us again with rules and paperwork. That separation cut deep. Some nights I would pick up the phone just to hear their voices, a small comfort against the strangeness of sleeping in a city of millions while feeling completely alone.

My older brother worked without rest. He found local jobs during the day and attended general education classes once a week, fighting to earn a certificate equal to a high school diploma so he could one day go to college. He understood exactly why we had crossed the ocean: for education, for stability, for a real future.

For me, everything changed the day I met a Vietnamese counselor at Walton High School. I was almost twenty years old and had been out of school for seven and a half long years, yet she still gave me a chance. She approved me for ninth grade.

I will never forget that moment.

I told myself something very clearly that day: This is the land of opportunity. I must seize education with both hands, because my parents risked everything so we could have this chance.

At first, I felt completely out of place sitting in ninth grade. I was the oldest student in the entire class. I felt awkward and embarrassed, my face burning every time someone glanced my way. But I kept going. I listened. I took notes. I studied late into the night.

Throughout high school I earned A or A+ in every math class. Numbers made sense to me when words did not. Even when English felt like an impossible wall, math remained clear, logical, and kind. It was the one place where I felt smart again, where my mind could run freely without stumbling over language.

And I was truly lucky. No one bullied me. In a new country, with a new language, starting school again from the beginning, being treated with simple respect was an enormous blessing.

I did not realize it then, but those quiet days at Walton High School were laying the first bricks of the life I would build in America — brick by brick, lesson by lesson, one solved equation at a time.

I still did not know where this road would lead. But I knew one thing: I had found my footing. And in mathematics, I had found the language that would carry me forward —

clear, honest, and patient, just like the compass that had once pointed us toward freedom.

Chapter 15

A SECOND FAMILY IN UPSTATE NEW YORK

Every two months I made the long trip upstate to visit my brothers, including Ánh, who was living with his foster family in Suffern. Each time the bus pulled into that small town, I felt like I could finally breathe again. Even though foster care and paperwork kept us apart, I held on to every chance to see him, my heart aching for those brief reunions.

One day, Ánh's teacher at Suffern High School introduced him to her husband's construction work. It was house remodeling — hard, honest labor. For two full summers before I finished high school, Ánh and I worked side by side whenever we could. We painted walls until our arms burned, hung sheetrock with nails that bit into our palms, fixed leaky faucets with cold water splashing our faces, and patched holes in old plaster. We learned real skills with our own hands, sweat dripping, muscles aching, but there was pride in every finished room.

Most nights I stayed at Ánh's house. His foster parents, Brian and Patricia Carew, never treated me like a visitor. They welcomed me as their own son. Every time I walked through their door, I felt a warmth I thought I had lost forever when I left Vietnam. The smell of home-cooked meals, the sound of laughter at the dinner table, the quiet way they asked about my day — it wrapped around me like a blanket I hadn't known I needed.

Little by little, I grew stronger. My English had improved. The fear that had lived inside me since the sea slowly faded. I began to feel more confident walking this new American life, one small step at a time.

◆

Brian and Pat often took us to visit their relatives during Thanksgiving and Christmas. For the first time since leaving Vietnam, I tasted something familiar again: family laughter, shared meals, and real warmth around the table. Those moments made me happy and heartbroken at the same time. Happy because I was loved. Heartbroken because I kept wondering where my parents and younger brothers and sisters were, and whether they were still alive. The joy was always threaded through with that quiet, persistent ache.

◆

As my courage grew, I did something I never imagined I would do in America. Sometimes I picked up the guitar and sang an English song for the whole family, the same song I had first learned back in the Bataan refugee camp: "How Can I Tell Her" by Lobo.

I sang with tears in my eyes, not from sadness, but from deep gratitude. Gratitude that I was still alive. Gratitude that someone was willing to sit and listen to a boy with broken English pour out his heart through a simple melody. The room would fall quiet, and in those moments, I felt truly seen.

◆

I will never forget Brian and Pat Carew. They gave me something priceless: the feeling of home in a foreign land. Their kindness became the bridge that carried me forward — in confidence, in education, in work, and in the life I was slowly beginning to build in America. I will carry their names in my heart forever.

Yet even with this second family surrounding me with love, one question never left my mind: Will my real family ever be whole again? That question had no answer yet. But for the first time, asking it did not feel like despair. It felt like hope.

Chapter 16

MY FATHER'S ESCAPE – THE FOURTEEN-DAY ORDEAL

My father had never driven a boat in his life, he did not know how to swim, yet he became the captain — without being given a choice.

One year after I reached America, my father decided to risk everything. Using the same careful planning that once carried me out of Vietnam, he quietly arranged his own escape in 1986. The experienced businesswoman who organized my journey in 1984 was the same woman who helped him now. This time, my father and my two younger sisters were simply passengers — "guests" on the trip. She promised she had hired a real captain and a mechanic. Forty people would board, including her own daughter, her brother, and the priest my father had been asked to look after.

The night before departure, my father sent the priest to the meeting house so he would not get lost the next day. A local security officer stopped the priest, questioned him for hours, and nearly ruined everything. That evening my father searched frantically until he found the priest back at his apartment, terrified and ready to quit. My father asked only for prayers — that the journey would begin within twenty-four hours and that God would protect all forty souls. Unexpectedly, the priest changed his mind. The next morning, they reached the meeting place safely.

Everything had been prepared: food, gasoline, supplies. All passengers were hidden under the cabin. Only the woman's son stayed above deck to steer the boat down the Thị Vải River toward the open sea. As they approached the river mouth, he turned to my father.

"Do you know how to steer a motorboat?"

"Never," my father answered honestly.

The young man gave him a ten-minute lesson, then jumped off onto his little rowboat and paddled back to shore to help his mother prepare the next escape.

◆

By 6:00 PM, about thirty nautical miles past Vũng Tàu, my father called out:

"Captain and mechanic — please come up and take over!"

People looked at each other.

For a moment, no one moved. The boat fell into an uneasy silence. When people realized there was no real captain on board, faces turned pale. A wave of fear spread quickly through the passengers. If no one knew how to steer the boat, how could they possibly reach the open sea?

My father himself felt a deep fear rising inside him. He could not swim, and the thought of falling into the open ocean terrified him. With a firm voice he said that if no captain stepped forward, he would turn the boat back to shore rather than risk everyone dying at sea.

No one answered. The two men had lied. They were just passengers who wanted a free ride. My father's voice grew firm:

"If we have no real captain, I will turn this boat back right now. I would rather go to jail than die at sea."

The moment he said "turn back," adults began to cry and beg. They pleaded with him to continue until at least they reached international waters. When my father asked who captain would be, every finger pointed at him. He had no choice. He became captain — unwilling, but determined, with the weight of forty lives suddenly on his shoulders.

He quickly gathered several young men and taught them how to read the map and compass — skills he had learned during my own escape the year before. They set a course for Singapore.

◆

The next morning, two Vietnamese fishing boats spotted my father's boat and chased it. Everyone panicked. The sound of their engines echoed across the water, growing louder as the distance between the boats slowly closed. Fear spread quickly among the passengers. Some whispered that the fishermen might report them to the authorities. A few people began to cry quietly, imagining prison waiting for them if they were caught.

My father felt the same shock and fear. He knew what prison meant for someone who had once served in the South Vietnamese army. But he forced himself to stay calm, gripping the wheel firmly. If they were captured this time, the punishment would be far worse. So, he focused only on one thing: keeping the boat steady and moving as fast as possible toward international waters. For the sake of forty lives on board, he refused to surrender to fear.

For several long minutes, the two boats chased them across the open water. My father's boat had a stronger engine, and little by little the fishing boats began to fall behind.

Suddenly someone shouted. The water container had slipped and rolled across the deck. Before anyone could grab it, it tipped over the edge and plunged into the sea with a heavy splash.

People rushed to the side of the boat, reaching out helplessly, watching as the container drifted farther and farther away. No one said a word. In that moment, everyone understood what had just been lost.

◆

By the second day they had nothing left to drink. From that moment on, thirst became their greatest enemy. By the third day, thirst began to torture everyone. Lips cracked and tongues swelled until speaking became difficult. Some people stared at the endless seawater around them with desperate eyes, but everyone knew that drinking it would only bring death faster. By day four the engine overheated and broke down completely.

People began drinking their own urine. Hope faded fast. At first, they prayed together; soon many were too weak even to pray.

My two sisters lay motionless, their strength gone. They begged my father to turn back.

"Yes... we will go back," he told them gently.

But inside, he refused to give up, his faith burning fiercely.

By the sixth day, the suffering had become unbearable. Everyone was severely dehydrated, lips cracked, tongues swollen, eyes sunken. Then, in the distance, a large ship appeared. It came close enough to see them clearly, but it did not stop to rescue. Instead, the crew lowered a hose, passing fresh water down to the desperate boat. For a few precious minutes, people drank greedily, water spilling over chins and chests, tears mixing with the stream.

But the boat had no containers strong enough to hold more than a few liters. The gift was fleeting. The hose was pulled back up. The ship sailed away. The small wooden vessel drifted on, engine silent, directionless, at the mercy of currents and wind.

The days blurred into one long nightmare. No engine. No fresh water. No land in sight. People vomited from weakness and despair. Children cried until they had no voice left. Adults lay still, staring at the sky, waiting for the end. Death felt very close — closer than hope.

◆

After eight days drifting under the burning sun, everyone was exhausted and critically dehydrated. No one could think clearly anymore — except my father. There was a metal toolbox on board. The engine was beyond repair, so the tools were useless. He threw the useless tools into the sea and kept the metal box. He washed it clean, then asked someone to wash the lid. By accident the lid slipped and sank.

For a second, hope died again.

My father stayed calm. He broke a piece of the cabin, cut a wooden replacement lid, and after several hours it fit perfectly. Something shifted. My father began preparing the box to boil seawater.

Later my father told us how he remembered that idea. When he was a boy, he had helped his older sisters cook rice wine at home. The process was similar. When the liquid boiled, steam would travel through a tube and cool into drops of clear water. In that desperate moment at sea, with everyone dying of thirst, that childhood memory suddenly came back to him.

So, he tried to recreate the same method using the metal toolbox, seawater, and a small tube. He filled the box with seawater, boiled it with the leftover gasoline, sealed it with the wooden lid, and inserted the small tube. Steam traveled through the tube and slowly condensed into fresh distilled water.

It was not perfect, but it worked.

The distilled water came out slowly, only a few drops at a time. Everyone watched those tiny drops fall as if they were watching life itself return. To them, each drop felt like a miracle.

Some people quietly wiped tears from their faces. Others waited silently for their turn, holding their cups with trembling hands. The priest stood nearby, whispering a soft prayer as he witnessed the first drops of fresh water fall into the container. At that moment, every drop of water meant another chance for someone on that boat to live one more day.

The acrid smell of gasoline, saltwater, and burning paint filled the air, making everyone cough. The cabin roof was gone and the sun burned their skin raw each day. Some poured seawater on their clothes, hoping it would preserve what little moisture their bodies had left.

Because the engine had failed early, they still had extra gasoline — an unexpected blessing that allowed them to keep the fire going day and night.

They collected only about two liters of water a day for forty people. Each person received just a few teaspoons. It was never enough. But it kept them alive, though in agony.

Yet my father never wavered. He kept everyone moving, kept them praying, kept them alive one teaspoon of distilled water at a time.

◆

By day ten, most were ravaged by dehydration. The boat drifted without direction, shaking violently with every wave. Still, they followed my father's commands.

On the fourteenth day, a ship appeared on the horizon. No one dared believe it at first. They watched for nearly an hour. It was a Filipino commercial ship. The crew had heard a major storm was coming and received permission to rescue the drifting boat. It was God's perfect timing.

Once aboard, each refugee was given a small cup of Pedialyte, then a small, sweet drink, and hours later a small bowl of beef porridge. Only later did they understand why the portions were so tiny: it was the safest way to feed bodies that had been starving for two weeks.

The priest's presence became a miracle of its own. No one spoke English, but the priest spoke Latin, and miraculously one crew member understood Latin. Communication was possible. On the second day they received proper meals, even beer.

By the end of that day, all forty souls were safely transferred to a refugee camp in Singapore. From there, the long wait began again — Singapore first, then Bataan. And finally, in 1987, my father and sisters stepped onto American soil. The ocean had taken everything from them. America would have to give it back.

They had drifted for nearly two weeks between life and death at sea. Freedom came at a great price.

Looking back now, I understand something I could not see as a child. My father was not just trying to survive. He was fighting to keep forty souls alive. Months later, someone took a photograph at Bataan. They are all smiling. After everything, they are smiling.

Bataan Refugee Camp, 1987. My two younger sisters are in the center of the front row, the priest stands in the middle row, and my father is behind him wearing a pink shirt.

The priest who had almost quit the night before departure — who changed his mind after prayer, who spoke Latin to the Filipino crew — did not leave the rescue ship in silence. He left a poem. Written in Vietnamese between June 1 and June 15, 1985, it is simultaneously a farewell to Vietnam, a prayer to Mother Mary, a thanksgiving after rescue, and a hidden memorial. Into its verses he wove forty capitalized words — one for each soul on the boat — so that no one who survived those fourteen days would ever be forgotten. My father has kept it for forty years.

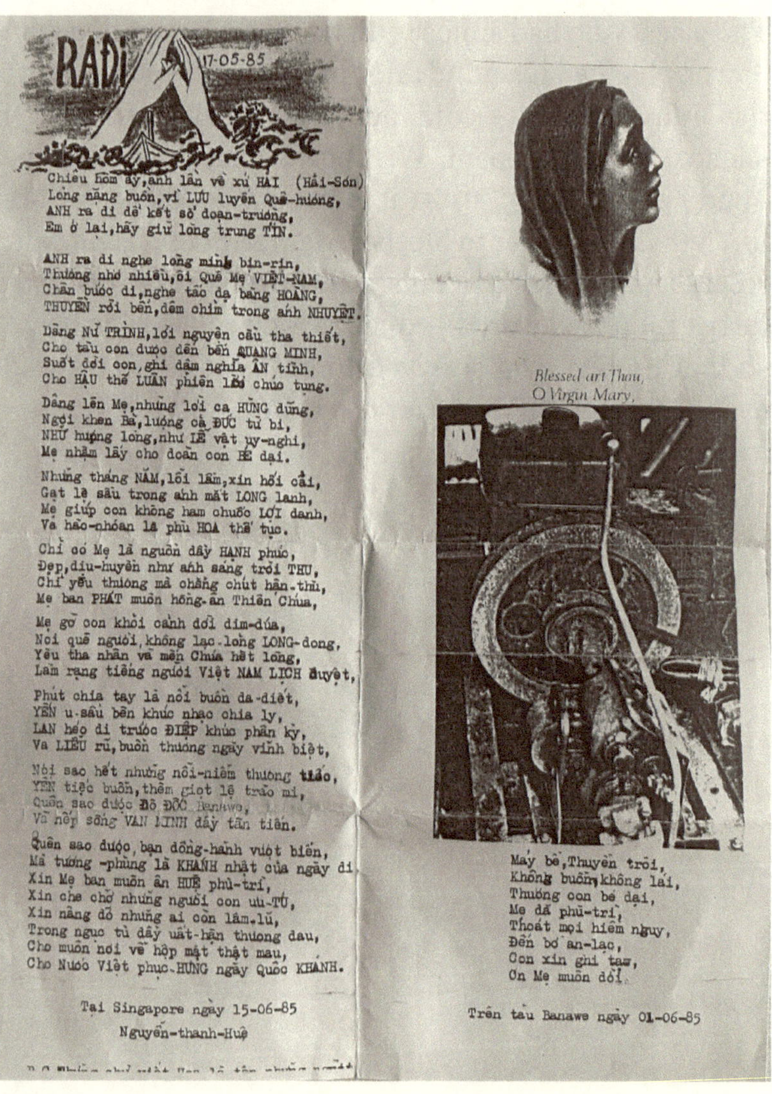

A poem written aboard the Filipino rescue ship Banawe, June 1, 1985, by Father Nguyễn Thanh Huệ. The forty capitalized names woven throughout the verses represent each survivor. The short prayer on the right was written on the day of rescue. The full poem was transcribed in Singapore on June 15, 1985.

English Translation

Translator's Note: The following is my best effort to render the meaning and spirit of Father Nguyễn Thanh Huệ's poem into English. As the poem was written in Vietnamese with names woven into its verses, a word-for-word translation was not always possible. Father Huệ passed away approximately ten years ago, and no formal translation was made during his lifetime. My father, who was present on that journey and was entrusted with the priest's care from the beginning, has given his blessing for this translation to be included here.

FAREWELL

(May 17, 1985)

This afternoon, my dear, I return to a distant land.
My heart grows heavy, remembering my homeland.
I leave to close a painful chapter,
You remain — keep your faithful heart.
I depart, hearing my heart quietly trembling,
Loving dearly, oh Mother Vietnam.
My footsteps echo across the vast sea,
The boat reaches shore, immersed in moonlight.
Virgin Mother, I humbly pray,
Guide Your children safely to bright shores.
My thoughts travel far, carrying bonds of love,
For future generations to offer praise.
Rising to Mother, these brave songs,
Praise offered in this letter.
Humbly, this simple gift,
Mother receives for Your children.
Through the years, I repent my faults,
Leave tears behind my calm gaze.
Mother helps Your child avoid fame and gain,
And the vanity of worldly flowers.
Only Mother is the source of happiness,
Shining like the autumn sun.
Love without hatred, Mother grants peace through God.
Mother lifts Your child from hardship,

Homesickness quiets in unity.
Love of homeland, trust in God,
Let the Vietnamese spirit shine.
The moment of farewell brings endless sorrow,
Soft sadness like parting music.
Lan follows first in this departure,
Liễu mourns this eternal goodbye.
How can we count all these tender memories?
Tears overflow in silent grief.
How can we forget Đốc and Banawe?
And the life of Văn Minh beginning anew?
How can we forget companions across the sea,
The joyful welcome of departure day.
We ask Mother for mercy and protection,
Shield Your devoted children.
Raise up those still struggling,
In captivity and suffering,
Let everyone reunite soon,
Let Vietnam rise again in freedom.

Singapore, June 15, 1985
Nguyễn Thanh Huệ

◆

Short Prayer
Blessed art Thou, O Virgin Mary.
Mother, the boat and engine struggle,
Do not abandon us.
Love Your little children,
Mother, guide us,
Through every danger,
To the shore of peace.
Your child writes this,
Forever grateful to Mother.

On the ship Banawe — June 1, 1985

The Forty Names

On June 1, 1985, the Filipino commercial ship Banawe rescued forty survivors who had been adrift at sea for fourteen days after departing Vietnam on May 17, 1985. Father Nguyễn Thanh Huệ, who was among them, marked the occasion with this poem — weaving each of their forty names into the verses as a living memorial. Those forty souls were: Ánh, Tín, Ánh, Nam, Hoàng, Trình, Minh, Luân, Ân, Hậu, Hùng, Đức, Như, Lễ, Năm, Lợi, Hoa, Tú, Khánh, Hạnh, Thu, Phát, Long, Nam, Lịch, Yến, Lan, Điệp, Liễu, Yến, Đốc, Minh, Khánh, Huệ, Tú, Nguyệt, Thuyên, Hưng, Hải, and Lưu. The name Khánh appears twice — once for my father, and once for a child on the same boat who shared his name. The priest's own name, Huệ, meaning grace, is woven in as well.

They all survived. By the grace of God, every single one.

Chapter 17

THE ESCAPE BY LAND – PHƯỢNG AND ÚT'S JOURNEY THROUGH CAMBODIA TO THAILAND

Phượng had just turned seventeen. Út was only seven years old. And together, they would survive things that would break most adults.

In 1987, after our father and two younger sisters had already reached America, our mother met a few Cambodian friends at church. Quiet conversations stretched late into the night until a dangerous plan slowly took shape. They believed they could guide Phượng and Út out of Vietnam by land. It sounded possible, but everyone knew death waited around every corner.

The route would take them by bus, on foot, and in tiny boats, slipping through Cambodia and then across one short river into Thailand.

With the help of those friends, Phượng and Út finally stepped into Phnom Penh, the capital of Cambodia. But the moment they arrived, every connection vanished without a trace. The people from the church were gone.

Nowhere to turn, Phượng and Út took shelter in the home of a local woman. She gave them food and a place to sleep while Phượng waited desperately for a boat that could carry them across the river into Thailand. Two weeks crawled by in gut-twisting fear. No signal came. Their money ran out. They could not even buy one more meal. Trapped and helpless, Phượng made the only choice left. She had to return to Vietnam.

◆

Before leaving, she met another woman nearby. They talked in hushed voices about a different route, a far riskier plan. The woman led her to a poor family that lived under a ragged tent on a scrap of land. Twelve souls — two parents and ten children — with no work and no money. Yet they owned a wooden boat big enough for about twenty people. The only problem was that it had no engine, not even for fishing.

After long whispered talks, Phượng felt her heart break for them. But she had no money to give. The father, Mr. Nam, spoke in a voice full of despair.

"If we had money for an engine, gasoline, and food, we could all leave together. Thailand would be only two hours away."

Phượng made a decision that tore her apart inside. She left little Út with another family for safekeeping, then slipped back across the border alone to beg for money from our mother. My mother gave Phượng every dollar she had. Without hesitation, Phượng turned and headed back toward Cambodia. On the road, she met a retired Vietnamese soldier who crossed the border often. He seemed calm and trustworthy. She paid him to guide her to the exact house where Út was waiting. Four long days later they arrived safely.

Eventually, Phượng followed Mr. Nam's plan. She handed him enough money for the engine, gasoline, and food.

With the help of his eighteen-year-old son, Mr. Nam prepared everything within a few days.

Twenty-one people climbed aboard: five adults and sixteen children. The youngest was only five years old. At that moment, Phượng realized she was no longer protecting just her little brother. She now carried the lives of twenty other souls on her shoulders. The younger children looked around with curious eyes, not yet understanding the danger. But the adults knew. In their silence hung the same question: would this journey lead to freedom — or the end of their lives?

◆

The boat pushed away from shore. Minutes later, a Thai patrol vessel appeared like a ghost ship, blocking their path. Guns pointed straight at their faces. Everyone raised their hands. Officers jumped aboard and shouted, "Are you Khmer Rouge?" No one spoke Cambodian. Everyone spoke only Vietnamese. The officers decided they were not Khmer Rouge and tossed them one pot of rice and one pot of soup.

Then horror struck. They ripped the engine off the boat and hurled it into the sea, then towed the boat a short distance, cut the rope, and left twenty-one helpless people drifting in the open ocean. Phượng had thought they were being rescued. Now, watching the engine sink beneath the waves, she understood the terrible truth.

Thailand did not want them.

As the engine was torn away, the metal base that held it in place ripped loose from the wooden hull. A gap opened where the engine had been, and seawater began seeping slowly into the boat. At first it was only a thin stream, but everyone quickly realized the danger. Even a small mistake could send the boat to the bottom of the sea if the water kept surging inside.

From that moment on, they took turns scooping water out with anything they could find — pots, bowls, even their bare hands — every ten minutes, day and night, trying desperately to keep the boat afloat.

With no engine and no direction, sudden panic swept through the group. Many wept and whispered, "We are going to die out here."

The fear was suffocating. Thai pirate boats hunted these waters every single day. If the little wooden boat drifted too close to them, they would swarm aboard, rape every woman and girl, then slaughter the men. The thought alone made her stomach twist with pure dread.

Phượng stood up in the middle of the chaos. She taught everyone a Vietnamese hymn so they could sing for hope and beg Mother Mary to watch over them in the deadly sea ahead.

"O Mother, shining Star, light my way as I journey across the sea of this life."

They sang hour after hour, day after day, while the boat drifted lost on endless water, praying they would see land before it was too late.

Phượng gathered scraps of cloth and sewed them into a makeshift sail. Instead of letting the boat drift to certain death, she turned it back toward land. She had learned that freedom demands action even when hope has run out.

A Thai fishing boat passed but offered no help. Another finally towed them to Coconut Island.

◆

The island was covered in coconut trees. The owner let them stay and gave them one sack of rice. But his wife warned them in a trembling voice, "On weekends the fishing boats come, and those men hunt women and girls to rape them."

Every time an engine sound echoed in the distance, the women and girls had to flee into the mountains, even though the jungle was dense, full of wild animals, and unknown dangers. Phượng hid with the others, choosing the terror of nature over the terror of men.

The first time, little Út fled into the mountains with Phượng, his small hand clutching hers amid the thick underbrush and swarming insects. But after they returned, Út fell gravely ill with malaria from the relentless mosquito bites, his tiny body wracked with fever and chills that left him weak and delirious. Phượng nursed him day and night, her heart aching as she wiped his brow and prayed for his recovery.

That weekend, the fishing boats returned, their engines roaring like predators in the night. The other women and girls ran for the mountains as before. But Phượng could not follow. Út was still burning with fever, too fragile to make the jungle climb. Leaving him alone was unthinkable. So she made a different choice — the only one left. She climbed a coconut tree fifteen feet high and sat frozen without moving for seven endless hours.

High above the ground, she could not twitch a single muscle. Ants crawled into her clothes and bit her skin. Mosquitoes feasted on her blood until the itch felt like fire. She bit her lip until it bled to stay silent. From her hiding spot, she watched the pirates dance around campfires, wave guns, and beat Mr. Nam's eighteen-year-old son and the other boys bloody, demanding to know where the women were hiding. The boys shook with fear but kept their mouths clamped shut. One sound, one scream would give the girls away. Her feet were numb. If the pirates spotted her in the tree, they would drag her down, and she would never be the same again. The horror of watching those young men take blow after blow while she sat helpless above them was something she would never forget.

◆

Two weeks later, Phượng and the others knew they could not stay. The island owner introduced them to another man who agreed to tow them somewhere else in exchange for their boat. That very night, they were taken to a deserted island blanketed in bright yellow Mai flowers (Ochna integerrima). It was three days before the Vietnamese and Chinese New Year, and the blooms glowed everywhere. The island looked like a painting, peaceful and empty.

But there was no food, no people, no shelter, and worst of all, the man had taken their boat and left them with nothing. No tools, no rope, no knife.

Staying meant certain death.

Phượng refused to let them give up. She urged everyone to gather dry wood, logs, floating trash, banana stalks, anything that could float. They built a raft that could carry three people at a time.

The next island lay approximately one kilometer away — lit windows, houses, and people visible in the distance.

For fourteen straight hours through the night, starving, exhausted, and terrified, they crossed that distance nine times, three people each trip. The first crossing began at five in the evening. The last one ended at seven thirty the next morning.

Three people climbed onto a wobbly raft made of sticks and vines. One person had to row the entire kilometer while the other two held on for their lives. Then one of them would row all the way back alone to bring the next two. Each trip took more than an hour.

If anyone slipped and fell into the water, even a strong swimmer would drown before reaching shore. The distance was too far, and the current too cruel.

Back on the empty island, the others waited in agony. They did not know if the raft had sunk, if their family members had already drowned, or if they would ever see them again.

Life and death balanced on the smallest mistake. One wrong wave. One loose knot. And the entire group could disappear.

Phượng could not stop thinking about it. The fear clawed at her chest throughout the night.

Yet she kept pushing everyone forward, never letting them see how terrified she truly was.

They survived because their courage refused to break.

◆

When they finally reached shore, local authorities pointed guns at twenty-one of them and accused them of being Khmer Rouge. After proving they were not, the group received food and was held for one week. The Red Cross was called, and papers were prepared.

After that camp, Phượng and Út were moved to two more refugee camps. Each transfer brought fresh fear, new surroundings, and another round of agonizing waiting. The final camp was huge and crowded, holding nearly ten thousand people from every background. Life there was hard, but hope held on. Phượng and Út stayed in that last camp for more than six months.

From the day they left Vietnam until the day they stepped onto American soil, more than two years had passed in tears and endless prayer.

After months of paperwork and interviews, our father was finally able to sponsor them through family reunification. At last, the long journey that had begun in terror slowly opened into a new life.

Their escape did not truly end when they crossed borders or survived the sea. It ended only after years of waiting, endurance, and unbreakable faith. That is the price of freedom — a price that can sometimes cost a person's very life.

1988, Phượng and Út, Phanat Nikhom Refugee Camp, Thailand.

Chapter 18

SETTLING IN – LEARNING, WORKING, AND THE EARLY AMERICAN YEARS

In the first years after arriving in the United States, while I was still in high school, my brother Ánh and I worked construction once a month on weekends in upstate New York. Our boss, Mr. S., owned many rental properties, so there was always something to fix. We painted houses, patched walls, replaced doors — whatever needed doing. The pay was modest, but the work gave us a sense of purpose and a little money to contribute.

After graduating from high school, government financial support ended. I had to stand completely on my own feet. I worked nonstop, always thinking about how to cover the next bill and how to continue my education.

When I started at Union College, I continued working while studying. My job was driving the campus shuttle van, taking students around the sprawling grounds. Classes filled my days, but between lectures and after them I drove to earn enough for food, books, and rent. Every dollar felt hard-won.

Later, during pharmacy school, weekends often found me working at Edo Japanese Restaurant as a busboy. The wage was only about five dollars an hour, but I was grateful for it. Occasionally, I still picked up small remodeling jobs to bring in extra cash.

Life in the land of opportunity was not easy. Those early steps on American soil were filled with hardship. Yet the years of studying while working taught me something no classroom could — that perseverance is built one hard day at a time.

◆

It was during one of those remodeling jobs near the Hudson River that something unexpected happened. After working alone at the site for about a week, I arrived one morning and noticed a car already parked in the driveway. I wondered who could be there so early. When I walked inside, I saw a girl standing by the window, carefully painting the frame. She was so focused on her work that she did not notice my presence at first.

I gathered my courage and introduced myself. Only then did I learn that she was Mr. S.'s daughter. He had never mentioned that she would be helping at the site.

Her name was Tammy. She was about eighteen years old — pretty, gentle, and soft-spoken. She had just finished high school and was preparing to leave for college. For a short time, she worked alongside me.

I was so nervous that I barely spoke to her. I even worried that the boss might fire me if he noticed us talking too much. But Tammy was kind. She smiled often and asked small questions. Every time our eyes met, my heart fluttered.

◆

One day after lunch, I finally found the nerve to ask if she would walk with me along the Hudson River. The sun was warm, a gentle breeze drifted across the water, and the scenery was beautiful. We walked slowly toward the river. The path was scattered with small stones, easy to trip on. Without hesitation, Tammy reached out and took my hand.

For a moment, the world around me seemed to disappear.

Her hand was warm and soft. I was deeply moved, yet I held her hand gently. I did not dare squeeze tighter or say anything more. I did not dare confess my feelings. I was afraid the boss might find out. I was afraid to ruin everything. My life in America was still too new and uncertain.

Before I left for Union College, I stopped by her workplace at the Nanuet Mall in New York to see her one last time. We hugged for a long moment. I gave her a light kiss on the cheek. It was our goodbye. Words seemed unnecessary. Tammy did not speak. She simply smiled sadly. I did the same.

That was one of the first times my heart had beaten so strongly since coming to America. It was also the first time I chose to remain silent.

◆

Though it never became more than that, the moment we held hands by the Hudson River remains one of the sweetest and purest memories of my early years in this new land. It left me with both sweetness and a lingering ache.

In that moment, I realized that freedom is not only about surviving.

Sometimes it also means learning to let go of beautiful things we are not yet brave enough to hold.

Those years of quiet perseverance, of unspoken longing, shaped the person I was becoming. In the land of opportunity, I was finding my footing — one equation, one shift, one heartbeat at a time.

Chapter 19

UNIVERSITY – WHERE THE DREAM BECAME REALITY (1989–1996)

After graduating from high school, I entered Union College to study computer science. It was supposed to be the next step toward the dream my parents had carried for so many years — to build a real future in this new country.

But Union College proved far more difficult than I had expected. Not because I lacked intelligence, but because my English was still too weak. I fell behind badly in courses that demanded heavy reading and writing. I even had to retake ESL classes on campus. I pushed as hard as I could, but the grades remained harsh: mostly Cs and Ds. Some nights, staring at those marks, I wanted to give up. Yet every time I thought of my parents' quiet hopes in those long nights in Đồng Tháp Mười, I forced myself to keep going, one painful step at a time.

There was one subject where I found solid ground.

Mathematics.

In Calculus 1, 2, and 3, I earned an A in each class. Numbers spoke to me in a language without confusion or fear. In math, I no longer felt lost. I felt a small piece of confidence return — something the war and the ocean had taken from me long ago.

◆

Even so, the pressure never lifted. Loneliness pressed in hard. I was helpless in many ways. In the entire school, I knew fewer than five other Vietnamese students. The campus was quiet to the point of heartache, yet I could find no peace inside it. I did not feel I truly belonged there. Many evenings I walked back to my dorm alone, wondering how long it would take before this strange new life would finally feel like home.

During the winter months at Union College, the snow would cover the entire campus. Especially in January and February, the view from my dorm room window was nothing but white. The trees stood silent under the snow, and the empty paths across the campus looked almost forgotten. I loved snow at first — it was something beautiful and new to me. But the cold that came with it made the loneliness even deeper. Few students walked outside. Most days I simply went to class and then returned quietly to my room.

Those were some of the saddest and most confusing days of my life. I could not even explain what I felt. It was a kind of nameless sadness. My studies were already difficult, and I had almost no one to share my struggles with. Going home to visit family was not easy either — it took four hours by bus, and I did not have a car. I was not completely hopeless, but I did not know what to do to comfort myself.

The counselor suggested I major in mathematics and become a teacher after graduation. But I could not accept it. I asked myself silently: How can I teach math in English when I still stumble over every sentence? For me, that path was impossible.

◆

So I made a decision that would change everything. I reconnected with old high school friends and transferred to Marie Schwartz College of Pharmacy in Brooklyn, New York — and from the moment I arrived, everything felt different.

I fell unexpectedly in love with the pharmacy field. I met more than ten Vietnamese classmates, some from California. We connected instantly. We studied in groups, lifted each other up, and pushed through every tough exam together.

During those years in pharmacy school, I also became more involved with the small Vietnamese student community on campus. At one point, I was elected president of the Vietnamese Student Association. We had around thirty members. Once a year, we organized a cultural event to share Vietnamese traditions with the school. The men performed songs, and the young women wore beautiful áo dài, the traditional Vietnamese dresses.

One year I organized a group trip for our members to see the Broadway musical Miss Saigon. Because it was considered an educational cultural activity, getting approval for the budget was not difficult. After purchasing the tickets, I brought everyone to the show together. It was the first Broadway performance I had ever seen in my life. Everyone was deeply moved by the story, and that night became one of the most memorable moments of our student years.

For the first time since leaving Vietnam, for the first time since stepping onto American soil, I felt something deep inside me: This is the place I belong to.

◆

I began the pharmacy program in 1991. At last, I was walking the path my parents had dreamed of for us from the moment they chose freedom: education, stability, and a real future.

Pharmacy school was not easy. The most brutal subject was Medicinal Chemistry. Nearly three-quarters of the class failed. It was not laziness or lack of effort. In my view, it was a teaching issue. The professor did not follow the book; he focused only on his favorite topics. That made the material chaotic, confusing, and discouraging — especially for someone like me, still wrestling with English and years of interrupted schooling.

I failed the course and had to repeat it. I took the class again, with a different professor, and everything shifted. I finally understood the material, and I earned a B+. That was one of the harshest lessons of my life — not only in chemistry, but in perseverance. Sometimes you fail not because you lack ability, but because the system itself is not fair. Even then, you must rise and try again.

◆

As graduation approached, I often found myself sitting quietly with my books, thinking about everything that had brought me to this moment. The journey had been long, painful, and uncertain — but it had not defeated me.

In 1996, I graduated with a BS in Pharmacy.

For a moment, I thought of the open ocean that had once carried me away from Vietnam. The waves that had nearly taken my life had somehow carried me all the way to this moment.

From Vietnam to the open sea, from refugee camps to the long struggle with English, loneliness, failures, and second chances — every step of that journey had led to this moment.

I did it.

And somewhere in my heart, I felt that my parents' long journey through the flooded fields of Đồng Tháp Mười had finally reached its shore.

1996 — Vietnamese New Year gathering. A sailboat hangs on the wall behind us. From left to right: me, Út, Hiền, Huy, Ánh, and Mom.

Chapter 20

THE TURTLE AT MIDNIGHT

In the summer of 1993, two years after I started pharmacy school, I was looking for a way to earn extra money before the next semester began. A friend mentioned salmon fishing in Alaska where the pay could reach a thousand dollars a week. The money was tempting. But the cold weather was not. I had survived enough hardship in my life — I was not going to spend my summer freezing on the Alaskan coast by choice.

Then my high school friend Khôi mentioned that his father, Chú Hùng, was planning a shrimping trip to Galveston, Texas. I said yes immediately. I trusted Chú Hùng and his family. And honestly, the idea of a long drive through different states appealed to me just as much as the work itself. I had always loved seeing America from the road — the changing landscapes, the different skies, the feeling of a country still revealing itself to me mile by mile.

Khôi drove down with me to Texas but stayed on shore while I went out with the crew for five days. It was an opportunity to earn a little extra money for the coming semester — something I always needed. At the time, I thought it would simply be a small adventure before returning to school. Part of me was also curious about life on the Gulf waters. Years earlier, the sea had nearly taken my life during our escape from Vietnam. Yet somehow, I still felt drawn back to it.

There were seven of us on the boat, including the captain. Most of the men were older and had spent years working the Gulf of Mexico. I was the youngest person on the boat — just a pharmacy student trying to build a future in America.

During the day, we worked under the hot Texas sun, pulling heavy shrimp nets from the water. The sea was full of life. We caught shrimp, crabs, and many different kinds of fish. Sometimes dolphins appeared beside the boat as if they were quietly guiding us through the waves.

◆

But after a few days on the boat, I began to experience a very different side of life at sea.

The men were tough people who had lived hard lives for many years. Their voices were rough and their tempers unpredictable. The conversations on that boat were not comfortable ones. I was the youngest person there and the only one who seemed uneasy with the atmosphere around me.

I quickly realized there were unspoken rules on the boat. The captain made the decisions, and everyone else followed without question.

As the days passed, I became more cautious. The rough language, the careless way problems were handled, and the tension in the air reminded me that I did not truly know these men. I was only a guest on their boat, far from shore and completely dependent on them.

◆

One afternoon, while pulling in a heavy net, we accidentally caught a large sea turtle.

The turtle struggled as the men dragged it onto the deck. Its flippers pushed helplessly against the wooden floor while its dark eyes looked around in fear and confusion.

Some of the fishermen became excited. The captain decided we would keep the turtle and cook turtle soup later. The others agreed without hesitation as they tied the turtle near the side of the boat.

I said nothing. But inside, one thought would not leave me: they had already caught more than enough — jumbo shrimps, varieties of fish, crabs piled high on the deck. Why the turtle?

Back in Vietnam, I had heard of people eating turtle. It was not unusual there. I also knew the old belief — that mistreating or killing a turtle would bring bad fate upon you. But that was not what troubled me. I did not want to save the turtle out of superstition or fear of consequence.

I saved it because it deserved to live its full life. That was reason enough.

Since coming to America, I had also learned that sea turtles were a protected species — animals the government worked hard to preserve. Catching and keeping one was not just wrong to me. It was illegal.

I stood quietly and watched the turtle for a long time. It had done nothing wrong. It had simply become trapped in our net. The more I looked at it, the heavier my heart became.

Years earlier, my own family had drifted helplessly across the South China Sea praying for mercy from strangers. Looking at the turtle lying there on the deck, tied and helpless, I saw something I recognized. Not just fear — but helplessness before the hands of strangers.

But I said nothing.

I knew speaking up would accomplish nothing. Deep in the back of my mind was a fear I could not ignore. I did not know these men well. We were far from shore. If they discovered what I had done, I did not know how they might react.

We were alone in the middle of the Gulf of Mexico.

So I stayed quiet.

But no matter how hard I tried, I could not stop looking at the turtle. Its slow movements across the deck, the ropes around its body, and the fear in its eyes stayed with me the entire evening. The others laughed, smoked, and continued their work as if nothing about it mattered.

But to me, it mattered.

A pair of dark, helpless eyes weighed on my heart so heavily that sleep became impossible until the turtle was free again.

And deep inside my heart, I already knew what I had to do.

◆

That night, after everyone finished eating and slowly fell asleep, I lay awake listening to the sound of the engine and the waves hitting the side of the boat. I could not stop thinking about the turtle.

Silently, I prayed. I asked God to help me save the turtle and protect me from being discovered.

Near midnight, I quietly stood up and pretended I was going to the bathroom. My heart was beating hard as I slowly walked toward the turtle. The deck was wet and slippery. Every small sound felt loud in the middle of the night. I kept looking behind me, afraid someone might suddenly wake up.

The turtle was heavy, and I struggled to push it quietly across the deck without making noise. Near the side of the boat was a large opening designed to let water escape during rough weather and high waves. Slowly, carefully, I guided the turtle toward that opening.

For a brief moment, the turtle stopped moving, almost as if it understood what was happening.

Then, with one final push, it slipped through the opening and disappeared back into the dark Gulf waters.

AI reimagined the night I helped rescue a sea turtle and return it to the ocean.

I stood there frozen in silence.

The ocean swallowed the sound completely.

For a few seconds, I simply stared into the darkness. Then I looked up at the night sky and whispered a quiet prayer of thanks before returning to my bed.

◆

The next morning, the fishermen were confused. They searched around the boat trying to figure out how the turtle had disappeared during the night. Some blamed the loose rope. Others thought the turtle somehow escaped on its own.

No one ever discovered what had happened.

I remained silent.

But deep in my heart, I believed He had watched over me that night.

Years earlier, my family had prayed for mercy while drifting helplessly at sea. On this night, in another sea under another dark sky, I felt that God had allowed me to return a small act of mercy to another living creature whose life was also hanging by a thread.

◆

When the trip ended, Khôi was waiting on shore. We packed the car with shrimp, fish, and dry ice to bring home to the family, and drove all the way from Texas back to New York together. It was a long drive, but we laughed and talked the whole way.

Somewhere out in the Gulf, beneath those dark waters, a turtle was swimming free again. And as the miles passed beneath our tires on the road back to New York, I carried

with me something that no paycheck from that trip could
ever equal.

Chapter 21

ONE PHONE CALL AWAY (1997–2001)

After graduating from pharmacy school in 1996, I did not begin my first pharmacist job in New York. My life still felt too unstable at the time. Instead, I chose California.

When I visited a friend in Orange County, I instantly fell in love with the sunshine. After years of snow, struggle, and survival, California felt like warmth returning to my life.

A pharmacy friend introduced me to a girl named Julie, who would later become my wife. He tried to arrange for us to meet when I came to visit for a week in the summer of 1997, but the meeting never happened.

Then, in early September 1997, my friend called me again. His voice was serious.

"You must call Julie. Otherwise, you will lose your chance."

I was confused. How could I talk to a girl I had never met, over the phone, from thousands of miles away? I was in New York and she was in California. What would I even say? How do you begin a love story with a stranger's voice?

But deep inside, something stirred. A new kind of fear —
not the fear of running from communism, but the fear of
stepping toward love.

I asked my friend to arrange the call. His name was Hùng,
and somehow, he had already done everything. He had
spoken to Julie's mother and told her good things about
me.

So, I called. Julie's mom answered first. I was terrified she
would not like me or would not understand why I was
calling. But she welcomed me warmly. She spoke with me
for about five minutes, then passed the phone to Julie.

There was a brief silence.

"Hi... this is Quang," I said, unsure of my own voice, my
fingers tightening around the phone.

She laughed softly. "I know. My mom just winked at me
and gave me a smile."

Even though we had never met before, her voice was so
sweet that it immediately attracted me. We talked about
simple things at first — where we grew up, what we were
studying, how strange it felt to speak to someone we had
never met. But even in those first few minutes, there was
an ease I could not explain. It felt as if we had known each
other much longer than a single phone call.

◆

We began talking every single day. Long-distance calls
then cost ten cents a minute, and we talked for an hour
and a half, sometimes two hours, every single night.
Whenever Julie called me first, I would tell her to hang up
— then I would call her right back. I wanted the bill to stay
on my side. Our phone bills climbed to three or four
hundred dollars each month, money I could not easily

spare. But we did not care. Through words, laughter, and growing trust, we built something real across the distance.

At the time I was working as a pharmacist intern at CVS. My brother Hoàng loaned me an old Pontiac whose heating system had long since stopped working. On cold nights I plugged a small portable heater into the cigarette lighter just to warm my hands while driving. It was cold and uncomfortable — but somehow I handled it without complaint. It was nothing compared to my escape mission.

After three months, I could not stay in New York any longer. On December 27, 1997, I flew from New York to California with a one-way ticket. At that time, I barely had enough money for the plane fare.

◆

I had already passed the North American Pharmacist Licensure Examination (NAPLEX) in New York, but California did not accept it for licensure. So when I arrived, I had to start the licensing process all over again. At first, I worked as an intern in a retail pharmacy while waiting for my California pharmacist license.

The California pharmacy board exam was extremely difficult. I did not know how to prepare, and I failed twice. Each failure hit harder than I expected. I had already survived war, the ocean, and years of struggle as a refugee. Yet here I was, defeated by an exam. After the second failure, I sat in silence, staring at the result as doubt slowly crept in. Maybe I was not good enough. Maybe I had reached my limit.

But then I remembered another moment — standing on a small boat in the middle of the ocean, when the engine died and panic could have ended everything. Back then, giving up was not an option. We had to think, adjust, and keep going. This was no different.

So I went back to study — not the same way as before, but with discipline, focus, and a deeper understanding of my weaknesses.

Life, however, did not pause to wait for me. While studying for the exam, I moved to Las Vegas for my first pharmacist job, working at a Walgreens pharmacy. I stayed there for about a year and a half. I chose Las Vegas because it was closer to California than most other states, making it easier to drive back when needed.

Through all of it — the long drives, the long shifts, the long nights of studying — I kept pushing. I took the exam again. This time, I passed.

◆

Working at Walgreens was an experience unlike anything I had known before. Customers came from all over the United States — tourists, travelers, locals — and every day brought something unexpected. I remember one moment during my second month there. The store manager rushed back to the pharmacy, his voice urgent and loud.

"There is a man on the floor trying to breathe!"

Without thinking, I grabbed an inhaler, jumped over the pharmacy counter, and ran toward the middle of the store. A man was gasping for air, his face pale with panic. I handed him the inhaler. He inhaled it. Within moments, his breathing steadied and color returned to his face.

It was like a miracle — a gentle reminder that my years of study and struggle had a purpose beyond myself.

◆

Every two weeks, I drove more than four hours one way to see Julie, who was living in Redlands, California at the time. The desert highway stretched endlessly in front of me, silent at night, with only the hum of the engine and the glow of distant headlights. Sometimes my eyes felt heavy and my hands tightened on the steering wheel, but the thought of seeing her kept pulling me forward. Those long drives never felt like a burden. Instead, they became moments of quiet anticipation — counting the miles until I could finally be with her again.

I remember one trip heading north on Interstate 15, the road sloping gently downhill, the pavement so smooth it almost felt effortless to drive. I moved with the flow of traffic, surrounded by four other cars, all of us traveling close to ninety miles per hour. In that moment, it felt normal — safe, even — because I was not alone.

A few miles later, after the road leveled out, everything changed. Two police cars appeared ahead, lights flashing. They began pulling over the cars in front of me, and then suddenly, I heard a loudspeaker call over me as well. I rolled down my window, confused.

"What's going on? I didn't even see you on the road."

The officer looked at me calmly and said, "You didn't see me. The helicopter saw you."

In that instant, my confidence disappeared. I nodded and said quietly, "Okay... give me the ticket."

Later, I attended a DMV class and paid the fee to remove the point from my license. It was a simple mistake, but a lasting lesson. I learned that following the crowd does not always lead you in the right direction.

Still, no matter how long or tiring those drives were, every mile brought me closer to Julie. Our time together was never long, but each visit strengthened our trust, our patience, and our hope for the future we were slowly building together.

◆

Julie and I got married on January 8, 2000. I remember standing beside her, my hands slightly trembling as I held hers, looking out at the small gathering of family and friends, and thinking how impossible this moment once seemed. Years earlier, we had only known each other through a phone line stretched across the country. Now she stood beside me, real and present, her hand in mine. For a brief moment, everything was quiet. No distance. No struggle. Just us, beginning a life together.

Even then, after the wedding, I was still driving back and forth between California and Las Vegas every two weeks. Julie was staying with her parents and working at Loma Linda University Medical Center as a sonographer.

Sometimes I felt that my entire journey had been one challenge after another — Vietnam, the open ocean, refugee camps, school, licensing exams, long-distance love, and endless miles on the road. But deep inside, I knew the truth: someone had been watching over me the whole time.

◆

Thank God, I finally passed my California pharmacy board exam in June 2001. The company I worked for transferred me back to California, and the new job was very close to my parents-in-law's home.

I still remember the day I left Las Vegas — September 11, 2001. That date would forever carry two meanings for me — one for the world, and one for my own life. On that same morning, America was shaken by the terrorist attacks that brought down the Twin Towers in New York City.

I was excited to finally begin our full life together in California. My wife and I bought a new home in Loma Linda, a place that soon became the center of our new beginning. After years of moving from one place to another, it finally felt like we had found a place to settle down and build our future together.

We have lived in that home ever since, watching our lives slowly take root there. In 2003, our greatest blessing arrived when we welcomed our lovely son, Andrew, into the world. His birth filled our home with new joy and purpose, marking the beginning of a new chapter for our family.

December 1997

Chapter 22

THE DAY THE DREAM BECAME WHOLE

As I held that diploma in my hands in 1996, a quiet wave of gratitude washed over me. The long battle for education — the late nights, the failures, and the many restarts — had finally borne fruit. I had proven to myself, and to the parents I still carried in my heart, that their sacrifices were not in vain.

Yet even in that moment of personal victory, one truth remained unshakable: my success was only half the dream. The other half — the dream my parents had whispered about through years of hardship — was the day our entire family could stand together again, whole and free.

After years of waiting and praying, the last piece of our family came together. In 1994, the last journey brought my mother and my youngest sister to America, sponsored by the rest of us. By 1996, all ten of us had finally reached American soil. But it was not until that year, on the day I graduated with a Bachelor's degree in Pharmacy, that the dream truly felt complete.

◆

The auditorium was filled with proud families, but none shone brighter than ours. There they were — my parents, my brothers, my sisters — all ten of us children together for the first time on American soil in one place.

My mother sat in the front row, tears streaming down her face, her hands pressed together as if in prayer as my name was called. My father, who had once captained a drifting boat through the jaws of death, now watched his son walk across the stage. My siblings clapped until their hands hurt, their smiles wide and unbroken.

When I stepped down from the platform, diploma in hand, we met in the aisle. We embraced tightly — a circle of twelve people who had once been scattered across oceans and borders, now finally standing together in one place. Our arms held on as if we were afraid this moment might slip away.

There were only tears, laughter, and the quiet knowledge that we had made it.

Even today, that moment returns to me with the same quiet fullness in my heart.

◆

My siblings went on to build lives across many fields — engineering, business, healthcare — each of us finding our own path in this new world. As for me, I chose the path of pharmacy and have been working in Loma Linda, California, for many years.

From the bottom of my heart, I thank God for guiding our entire family safely through every danger — every moment when we could have lost our lives. We rebuilt our lives on this new soil with nothing but our own two hands.

On behalf of my whole family, I express our deepest gratitude to the United States — the country that opened its arms and welcomed refugees like us. From that day forward, we studied hard, worked tirelessly, and pushed ourselves forward so that we would never betray the trust this nation placed in us.

We will forever remember the United Nations, which stood by us from the middle of the vast ocean all the way to the shore of freedom.

◆

When I look back on the journey, I often sit quietly and reflect. Being a refugee is not only about facing giant waves, hunger, thirst, and the fear of death at sea. In many ways, the hardest part begins after you reach the land of opportunity.

That is when you must learn how to build a real home again in a new country, with a new language and a new culture. Starting from absolute zero, we had to plant every seed ourselves and nurture every dream ourselves, proving day after day that we deserved to stand here and shine.

All the sweat, the long nights, and the moments when we wanted to give up — every one of them was worth it. Those struggles shaped the people we have become today.

That boy who once watched his world disappear did not know, then, that he was already learning how to build a new one.

1996, Graduation from pharmacy school.

Chapter 23

THE YEARS WE LEARNED TO LOVE AGAIN

After the joy of reunion in 1996, we quickly discovered that coming together was only the beginning. The real challenge was learning how to live as a family again in a brand-new country.

Each of us had to learn to stand on our own feet. Our parents worked long hours just to survive, so we had to find our own paths — going to school, finding jobs, paying bills, and building a future in a place where we barely spoke the language.

◆

My oldest brother Thành took a full-time eight-to-five job while attending night classes to earn his GED. For years he worked all day and studied all night, sometimes driving a taxi just to make ends meet. Eventually he earned a degree in aeronautics and later found a stable IT position at Beth Israel Hospital in New York.

Ánh graduated from Union College with a degree in civil engineering and later moved to San Diego in 2000. There he built a life he loved, working during the day and fishing on the ocean in his free time.

Phượng, who had bravely led twenty people through Cambodia and Thailand at only seventeen — the girl who climbed a coconut tree for seven hours to survive — later opened her own successful business after finishing college. In the years after our mother passed away in 2023, she became one of the main reasons we still gather every year for a family reunion.

Hoàng and Huy both earned degrees in electrical engineering. Even today we still laugh about the morning Huy asked to turn the boat back because he had forgotten his crickets.

Hoa, who endured the fourteen-day ordeal at sea with our father, earned a business degree and has worked in accounting for many years. She loves to travel and often says America gave her the freedom to live the life she once only dreamed about.

The twin sisters also found their own paths — one became a sonographer in the medical imaging field, while the other earned a degree in computer science and built a long and stable career.

Út, our youngest brother who escaped with Phượng at only seven years old, went on to earn a college degree. He worked in IT for many years and later became a realtor. He often jokes that after surviving the sea and the jungle, selling houses should be easy.

◆

Even after our reunion, life was not always easy. Work, school, distance, and old misunderstandings slowly pulled us apart. Many of us carried quiet hurt and resentment in our hearts — old silences that had calcified into distance without anyone quite knowing when it happened. Conversations became polite but distant. We had survived the ocean together, yet we were emotionally drifting on dry land.

It was painful in a different way.

Then came the turning point.

A few days before our mother passed away on November 18, 2023 — the woman who had held this family together through floods, separations, and decades of waiting — we made a promise in her hospital room: we would never stay angry with one another again. We would choose love over pride and forgiveness over resentment.

We have kept that promise.

Every year since then, we gather for a family reunion. We also meet online once a week to pray and talk together. Those moments have slowly healed old wounds. We are learning that being family means choosing each other again and again — even when it is difficult.

◆

Looking back now, I understand something clearly.

The hardest journey was not the one across the ocean.

The hardest journey was learning how to love each other again once we had finally reached safety.

The sea once tried to scatter us across the world. But time, faith, and forgiveness slowly brought us back together.

And by God's grace, we are still walking that journey — together.

2023 — The ten siblings, from left to right: youngest to oldest Út, Hậu, Hiền, Hoa, Huy, Hoàng, Phượng, Ánh, Quang, & Thành

Chapter 24

PAT AND BRIAN

Years after we escaped the sea, I came to understand that survival does not end with rescue. Sometimes it continues in the quiet kindness of strangers who open their homes and their hearts — and in doing so, become family.

Pat and Brian were two of those people in our lives.

They were the adoptive parents of my brother Ánh. Their presence opened a new chapter for him in a foreign land. When Ánh first arrived in America, our family only knew that he had been sponsored by a family, but we did not yet know who they were. Everything about this new life felt unfamiliar to us.

Looking back now, I believe it was part of God's quiet plan. Pat and Brian did not have children of their own, and they chose to sponsor a refugee. In time, they became an inseparable part of our family.

◆

At first, everything between us felt new and uncertain. We spoke different languages, came from different cultures, and had lived very different lives. Yet kindness has its own language. Through simple meals, small conversations, and time spent together, the distance between us slowly disappeared.

Our cultures were different in many ways. In our Vietnamese family, meals were lively and full of conversation. At Pat and Brian's home, dinners were quieter and more relaxed. At first, many things felt unfamiliar to us — the food, the routines, even the way people spoke around the table. But over time, those differences became something we learned to appreciate. Their home taught us not only how Americans lived, but also how kindness could make strangers feel like family.

Over time, Pat even began learning how to cook a few Vietnamese dishes from Ánh. One of her favorites was beef with broccoli. Whenever we came to visit, she would often go straight to the market to buy fresh beef and broccoli and cook it for us herself. Small gestures like that made us feel deeply welcomed in their home.

◆

All my siblings grew very fond of Pat and Brian. For me, the bond was especially close. During my high school years, I often stayed at their house, sometimes at least once a month. On weekends, Ánh and I worked together painting houses or doing small repair jobs to earn a little money. Those were our first small steps in building a life in this new land.

Their home became a place where we continued to grow, study, and learn how to live in America. Being close to an American family taught us many things — how people lived, how they thought, and how everyday life worked in this new country.

In those early years, Pat especially liked the idea of me learning to play the guitar. She often said I had talent and encouraged me to pursue music. But I always told her that I only played for enjoyment, especially during quiet or lonely moments. In the end, I chose the path of becoming a pharmacist.

◆

There was also an interesting coincidence connected to music. When I was in the Bataan refugee camp, I often played the song Hotel California by the Eagles on my guitar. Then, on my very first day in America, Brian reached over to a small shelf in his living room and pulled out a few cassette tapes.

"You might like these," he said with a smile.

They were albums by the Eagles — exactly the music I loved. He also introduced me to Billy Joel. I was thrilled. Perhaps there had always been a small musician somewhere inside me, but I never imagined music would become my profession.

Still, the guitar remained a quiet part of my life. Every weekend, I play music in a Vietnamese choir. For a couple of years, I also played guitar with an American choir near where I lived. Sacred music has always brought a special peace to my heart, calming my thoughts after the many struggles of life.

One evening during a family gathering at their home, I picked up the guitar and sang How Can I Tell Her by Lobo — the same song I had first learned in Bataan, the same song I had practiced again and again not knowing where I would one day sing it. The room fell quiet. Pat smiled. I understood then that this was exactly the moment that song had always been waiting for.

Brian also loved playing the guitar. Sometimes we would sit together, playing and singing, especially during holidays. Those moments were simple but warm and meaningful.

After he retired, Brian often brought his guitar to senior living centers, where he entertained elderly residents. He loved sharing music with them, and you could see the joy on their faces as they listened and sang along. For Brian, music was never about performing. It was simply his way of bringing a little happiness to others.

◆

Our families often gathered for major holidays such as Easter, Christmas, and Thanksgiving. I still remember the Easter celebrations when everyone laughed together while searching for hidden eggs in the yard. Small moments like those slowly wove our lives together like one family.

After Ánh and I moved to California, Pat and Brian often visited him in San Diego and would stop by to see us in Loma Linda as well. During those trips, they also made time to visit my two other brothers, Hoàng and Huy, in San Jose. As more of us settled in California, Pat and Brian gradually began exploring more of the Golden State. They seemed to enjoy the warm weather and the familiar feeling of seeing our family again, and perhaps that was why we started seeing them more often.

About eight years ago, when Ánh turned fifty, he organized a large birthday celebration. Friends and family gathered, and of course Pat and Brian were there. It felt like a true reunion — two families brought together again to celebrate the long journey we had all shared.

◆

In 2022, Brian quietly left this world. When I heard the news, I felt a deep stillness inside me — as if a gentle song had ended.

Now only Pat remains. We keep in touch often, because to us she is no longer just a sponsor from long ago. She has become like a mother in our family.

Over the years, the line between sponsor and refugee quietly disappeared. What remained was something much simpler and much stronger — family.

When I think of Brian now, I often picture him with a guitar in his hands, playing gentle songs and bringing quiet joy to the people around him.

In the long journey of refugees like us, there are hands that reach out at the right moment to help us stand again on new ground. Pat and Brian were those hands in our lives.

Some people enter your life only once, but their kindness stays with you forever.

2018, Pat and Brian at Ánh's 50th birthday

2018, Pat and Brian with our family reunion at Ánh's 50th birthday

2004, Pat and Brian together with all of us at Hiền's wedding

2004, Brian plays guitar at Hiền's wedding

2015, Family reunion

Chapter 25

THE QUIET STRENGTH OF MY PARENTS

Long before we crossed the ocean, the courage that carried our family forward had already taken root in the lives of my parents.

When our family began a new life in America, my parents started over with very little. Like many refugees, they arrived with no wealth — only determination, faith, and the hope that their children would one day have a better future.

My mother worked six days a week as a seamstress in a dry-cleaning shop. Her days were filled with clothing and fabric, carefully repairing or adjusting garments so they would fit properly and look their best. She hemmed pants, altered dresses, fixed broken zippers — careful, patient work that suited her perfectly. Between customers she helped manage the dry-cleaning orders, making sure every garment was returned neat and well cared for.

My father worked tirelessly. He owned a small fruit cart and woke up every morning at three o'clock to prepare the fruit for the day. Before sunrise he carefully arranged oranges, bananas, apples, strawberries, and kiwi stacked in colorful rows so the cart would look bright and inviting to the people passing by.

No matter the weather — rain, cold, or the heat of summer — he made sure the cart arrived at its spot near the World Trade Center by seven o'clock every morning.

At other times he helped prepare egg rolls, frying them fresh and selling them to people walking by. These were simple ways to earn a living, yet he approached them with patience and quiet dignity.

Sometimes when I visited him, I would see the fruit stacked neatly while my father stood behind the cart greeting customers with a calm smile. It was not a large business, but he took pride in doing his work well.

Even at home he was rarely idle. If something was broken, he fixed it. If something needed cleaning, he took care of it. Staying busy seemed to give him peace.

Whenever he had the chance, he also joined charitable activities at church. Helping others was simply part of who he was.

◆

One memory from those years remains especially vivid — September 11, 2001. I said goodbye to Las Vegas as I began my return to California.

Before leaving the city that morning, I drove to the home of a close friend who had worked with me at Walgreens. I wanted to say goodbye before starting the long drive west. When I arrived, he told me to look at the television.

"What's going on?" I asked.

"Just look at the TV," he said.

I stood there watching the screen, trying to understand what I was seeing. Slowly it became clear that something terrible was unfolding. Two planes had crashed into the

World Trade Center towers in New York. America was entering a moment of shock and confusion that would change the country forever.

Then I remembered where my father often worked. That morning he and a few friends were selling fruit from a small cart near Wall Street in Lower Manhattan, only about half a mile from the World Trade Center — just as they had done on many ordinary mornings.

I quickly dialed my father's number. My hands suddenly felt cold. For a moment the phone only rang. I stood there staring at it, afraid of what I might hear.

When he finally picked up, his voice was still shaken. He told me that when he heard what had happened and saw the panic around him, he ran as fast as he could to escape the falling debris from the collapsing buildings. By God's grace, he made it out safely. For a long moment after hanging up the phone, I simply stood still and breathed.

◆

My mother carried a different kind of strength.

After working long hours as a seamstress in a dry-cleaning shop, she returned home and devoted herself to caring for the family. She cooked, shopped for groceries, and made sure all of us were fed. In our home there was almost always food waiting on the table.

There is one small moment I return to often. After school I would walk through the door and immediately smell the warm scent of home cooking filling the kitchen. My mother would already have dinner prepared — fresh rice, a bowl of soup, and often a simple dish of braised fish. Steam rose gently from the bowls.

She never asked for thanks. She would simply smile and say,

"Eat first. You must be hungry from school."

At the time it felt ordinary. Only later did I understand how much love was hidden in those simple meals.

◆

After retirement, my mom loved gardening. In the yard she planted gourds, squash, and fruit trees, just as she had done for many years in Vietnam.

In the early mornings she would walk slowly through the garden, touching the leaves and checking the growing fruit. Sometimes she carried a small basket, quietly gathering what had ripened. On some visits I joined her, helping harvest the vegetables and fruit she had carefully tended.

The garden was never large, but to her it felt like a piece of the life she once knew in Vietnam.

In the years before she passed away, she continued planting vegetables and fruit each season. When the harvest came, she would ask one of us to drive her to church on Sundays. After mass she would sell the vegetables and fruit she had grown. When everything was sold, she would carefully fold the bills and place them inside a small envelope. Then she would place the envelope into the hands of the church.

Acts of charity like that brought her great joy.

Watching her do this, I came to understand that the garden she loved was not only feeding our family — it was also nourishing her faith.

◆

Sometimes when I think about those years, small images from my parents' daily lives return to me. I see my father standing behind his fruit cart on a busy Manhattan street, greeting people as they pass while carefully arranging the bright oranges and apples that glowed under the early morning sun. I see my mother working patiently in the dry-cleaning shop, sewing, and repairing garments.

Their work was humble, but it was steady and honest. Through long days and early mornings, they slowly rebuilt a life for our family in a new land. Step by step, through quiet dedication and perseverance, they laid the foundation that allowed all of us to move forward and dream again.

The courage that carried us across the ocean did not begin on the boat. It began long before that — in the quiet strength of my parents.

In many ways, everything we have become grew from the seeds they planted.

2022, Mom's charity work after church, sharing vegetables from her garden.

2015, My parents

1983, My family after my third brother Ánh escaped the country.

Chapter 26

TWO STORIES FROM THE VA HOSPITAL

My parents taught us that true happiness comes more from giving than from receiving. These two moments from my work at the VA showed me what that lesson looks like on an ordinary day.

The Shoes That Restored Dignity

About nine years ago, I was working at the VA. It was a normal day — the kind that starts like any other: busy schedules, responsibilities, people coming and going.

Then the doorbell rang.

I walked over and answered it. Behind the thick glass window stood a male Veteran. His clothes were worn, and his face carried the heavy tiredness of someone who had been fighting life alone for a long time.

I'll be honest — before I opened the door, I hesitated. For a brief moment, I didn't feel completely safe. He looked homeless, and I didn't know his situation, his mood, or what he might do. My mind wanted to stay behind the glass where it felt protected.

But something in my heart pushed back and reminded me: this is still a human being standing in front of me.

So I opened the door and stepped out into the hallway to listen to him more clearly.

When I got closer, he showed me his foot. It was swollen and painfully squeezed inside his shoe. The shoe looked too tight for him, almost like it belonged to someone else. He told me he was in pain.

I offered to bring him inside and guide him to the right office where he could get medical help. But he shook his head and told me something that hit my heart:

He had already gone. And nobody cared.

In that moment, I knew I might not be able to fix everything for him. But I could still do something.

"Let's get you a pair of shoes that fit."

Before we left, I turned to my pharmacy technician, who had witnessed everything, and said: "Please let the team know I am walking with a veteran upstairs to the VA shop." Then we went.

I helped him choose a pair of shoes that would actually support his swollen foot — shoes that wouldn't punish him with every step.

In that moment, I wasn't thinking about how he looked. I wasn't thinking about what other people might assume. I was thinking about one thing: this man served our country. And today, he needed help walking.

So I paid for the shoes.

I didn't do it for recognition. I didn't do it so people would think I was a good person.

I wished him good luck and hoped his pain would ease. Then I returned to work.

Later that day, when I went home, I told my wife what happened. She listened carefully and agreed: what I did was a good deed.

But deep inside, I felt something even more meaningful than doing a good deed.

I felt reminded of my purpose.

◆

The Kindness That Fixes Things

In December 2025, I was working at the VA as a discharge pharmacist. On that day, I was supporting a team of nurses and doctors, and we were preparing a patient to go home.

The patient was in a wheelchair. He had been admitted to the hospital, received care, and now he was ready to be discharged. Everything was moving forward normally — until a message went out: his wheelchair was broken. And because of that, he could not safely go home.

To some people, a broken chair might sound like a small inconvenience — something that could wait. But when I read that message, something inside me didn't feel right.

If his chair is broken, then his freedom is broken. And if his freedom is broken, then going home isn't really going home.

So I messaged the team and offered: "I can take a look and see if I can fix the problem."

The nursing team responded: "No, it's okay." They were busy. But even after that message, I still couldn't ignore it.

I just wanted the patient to leave the hospital safely — with dignity.

So I went up to the patient's room alone first. I spoke to him about his discharge medications, answered his questions, and then looked carefully at his wheelchair.

The patient explained something that made everything clearer. He told me he needed his old chair because it had an electric drive unit — a feature that helped him move around without using all the strength in his arms. Without that electric drive, he would have to push himself everywhere with his hands, and that simply wasn't realistic for him.

That was the moment I understood.

This chair wasn't just a chair. It was his independence. It was his ability to move without pain. It was his ability to live.

I looked more closely and realized the problem was mechanical — missing or damaged screws. So I went downstairs to the VA electric shop — a place I had never visited in fifteen years of working there. The gentleman at the shop introduced himself as Richard.

"I didn't know we had our own electric shop after fifteen years of working here," I told him.

He smiled. "Yeah, we've been here forever. You can come down anytime for any fixing."

He spent about fifteen minutes searching and gathering a complete set of screws that matched what the wheelchair needed. When he handed them to me, it felt like more than tools in my hand.

"I made another important friend today," I told him.

He nodded. "You did."

It felt like a door opening.

I returned to the pharmacy and informed my team that I had found the parts and needed to go install them in the patient's wheelchair — so they would know I might be away longer than a regular counseling visit.

At that moment, my pharmacy resident Vincent looked up. "I want to go with you."

Together we went back up to the patient's room and began assembling the wheelchair carefully. We tightened the parts, made sure everything aligned, and checked it again and again until it felt stable.

When we finished, the wheelchair looked almost new.

The patient's face changed immediately. He looked relieved. He looked hopeful. He looked ready. He was happy — not only because the chair worked again, but because someone cared enough to try.

I took a picture and sent it to the team, simply to let everyone know the patient could safely be discharged and didn't need to stay another night in the hospital.

The response from the team surprised me. People sent hearts. People thanked me. People appreciated the effort.

But the truth is, I didn't do it for the praise.

I did it because in that moment, kindness was the right thing to do.

A Captain in Service, A Life of Purpose

Chapter 27

LETTERS TO MY SON

My dear Andrew,

When I look back on my life, I see how much of it was shaped by your grandparents — their courage, their sacrifices, and the quiet way they lived each day.

Now, I realize it is my turn to pass those lessons on to you.

I'm writing this on a quiet Saturday morning in March 2026, while the coffee is still hot and the house is silent. You're a grown man now, with your own dreams and your own path ahead. I don't know if you'll read these words when I'm gone, or if you'll one day find them tucked in the back of this book. Either way, I want you to know what I've learned, not from books, but from waves, from hunger and nights when the engine died and we thought the sea might take us.

I still remember the days when you were small, running through the house and asking endless questions about the world. Even then, I hoped you would grow up in a life far safer than the one we came from.

Freedom isn't free. We paid for it with every tear your grandmother cried while waiting five months for news of Phượng and Út. We paid with fourteen days adrift, no land in sight — only prayers. We paid with failing grades, long drives, and jobs that broke our backs. America gave us the chance to begin again, but nothing after that came easy. We fought every inch. So, when you feel like quitting because school is hard or work is unfair, remember: your grandfather steered a boat with no experience. You can steer your life with a little more.

Family isn't perfect. We argued after the reunion. We drifted. We said things we shouldn't. But we came back, because love isn't the absence of pain; it's the choice to stay anyway. So, if you ever feel angry at someone you love, go back. Say sorry. Hug them. Don't let pride win.

Faith isn't loud. Your grandfather didn't pray fancy words out on that boat. He just whispered, "Please don't let us die." And God answered, not with thunder, but with a hose of fresh water from a passing ship. During my own suffering the night before our rescue, as I wrestled with the waves and the storm, God calmed the fury of the sea, and dolphins appeared right when we needed hope. So, when life feels overwhelming, don't wait for miracles. Just keep talking to Him. **He** listens.

And most importantly, I love you. Not because you're perfect. Not because you succeed. I love you because you're mine — because you carry a piece of that boat, that jungle, that promise we made before your grandmother died. I have watched you grow from a small boy into the man you are today, and that has been one of the greatest blessings of my life. You don't have to cross oceans. Just cross the room when someone needs you. That's enough.

If I could give you one thing, it would be this:

Live like your life is hanging by a thread — because once — it was. And we didn't let go.

Dad

2017— The choir and me at our Vietnamese parish.

2014, My family

Chapter 28

THE PRICE OF FREEDOM

After all the stories of survival and reunion, one truth still haunts me after decades. It is time I speak it plainly.

More than one million Vietnamese people fled by sea after 1975. We call them the boat people. But behind that number lies a tragedy few people today fully understand.

No one knows exactly how many died. Historians estimate between 200,000 and 400,000 lives were lost in the South China Sea. Some believe the real number was even higher. They perished in violent storms, from thirst and starvation when engines failed and boats drifted helplessly for weeks, and — most brutally — at the hands of pirates who hunted these waters without mercy.

In 1981, the United Nations High Commissioner for Refugees recorded a single year that revealed the nightmare. Of 452 refugee boats carrying 15,479 people that reached Thailand, 349 had been attacked by pirates — an average of three times each. In total, 228 women were abducted and 881 people were reported dead or missing.

The new Vietnamese government often reacted to escape attempts with violence. Communist patrols waited along the narrow rivers leading to the coast, opening fire on families in boats trying to flee. Many never even reached the open ocean.

They knew the risks. Every person who stepped onto a boat understood they might never see land again. They understood they could be robbed, raped, murdered, or left to die slowly under the burning sun. Yet they still went.

Some survived horrors almost beyond words. One boat carrying seventy-five refugees was sunk by pirates. Only one person survived. Another boat lost most of its twenty-one women — abducted and never seen again.

One story has never left my mind. A boat from a village near ours drifted for more than three weeks with no food and no fresh water. When a small child died from hunger and dehydration, some adults, in their desperation, made the unthinkable decision to eat part of the child's body. That boy was the son of a family my parents knew well. The story was only whispered among survivors.

I once read the account of a refugee boat that drifted for seventeen days and was attacked by Thai pirates three separate times. Each raid brought the same nightmare: pirates swarming aboard, stealing everything of value, raping the women, and beating or killing any man who tried to resist. After each attack, the pirates left the broken boat drifting again on the open sea.

Everything was gone: food, water, gold, even dignity. Yet the boat continued drifting.

Finally, after the survivors had lost almost everything, another fishing boat appeared. This time the fishermen were not pirates. They took pity on the shattered vessel and pulled the survivors aboard, bringing them at last to a refugee camp in Thailand.

Those who lived through such nightmares carried scars no one could see. But they also carried something else: proof that even in the deepest suffering, the human will to live can refuse to die.

I survived that ocean. Many others did not.

That is the true price of freedom.

◆

This book is not written only for those who survived. It is also written in memory of those who did not.

The ocean that carried us to freedom also became the grave of thousands whose names history may never record.

No memorial marks the place where they disappeared.

No gravestones bear their names.

Only the **sea** remembers them.

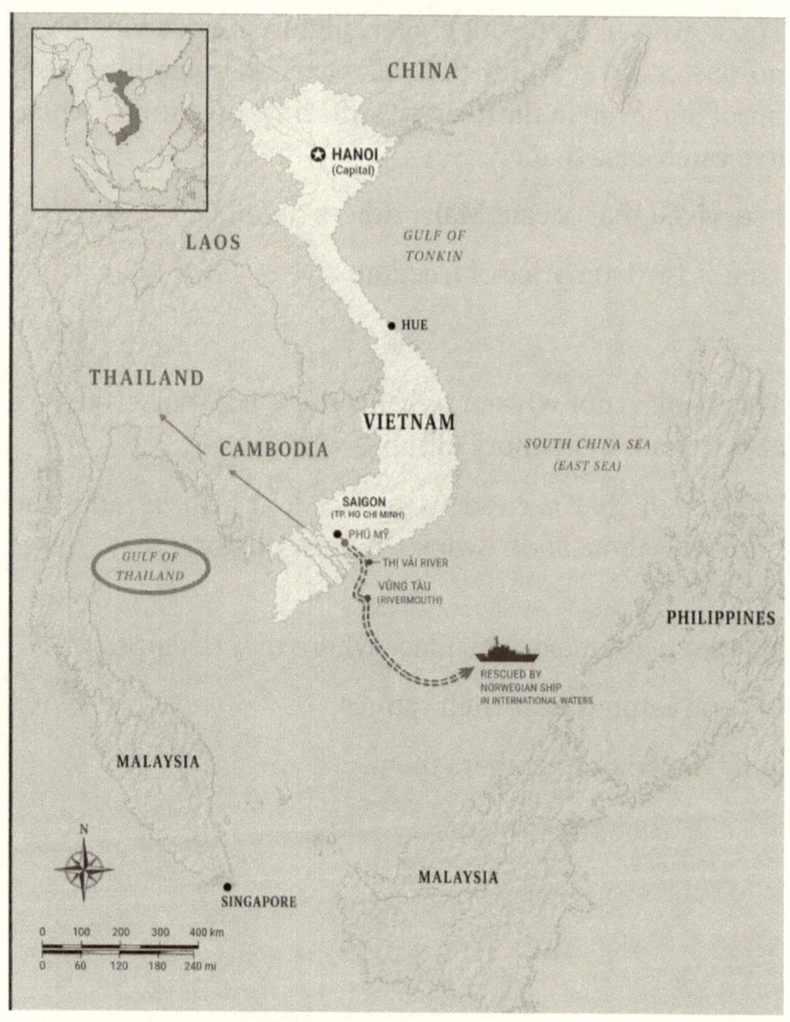

*Vietnam is shown in orange, shaped like the letter "**S**." Escape boats followed the **downward arrow** toward Southeast Asia—Malaysia or Singapore—across the South China Sea. When engines failed, winds and currents often pushed them into the Gulf of Thailand—the most dangerous waters—where many boat people faced starvation, pirates, and death. The **upward arrows** trace the land routes through Cambodia into Thailand taken by those who fled on foot.*

A Tribute To

PHƯỢNG

There are people in every family whose courage holds everyone else together — people who carry more than their share without complaint, without recognition, and without fully understanding, in the moment, how extraordinary they truly are.

Phượng was seventeen years old when she became that person for our family.

She left Vietnam with one small brother in her hand and nothing else she could count on. Unlike the rest of us, she had never sat around the lantern studying maps. She had never learned the fishing routes or practiced reading a compass. She was only thirteen in 1983, when our family was quietly preparing to escape — too young to be included in those careful, whispered circles of learning. She knew nothing of navigation, nothing of the sea.

What she had was something no map could give her.

She had listened. During the years our family used a sailboat along the coast, she paid quiet attention — how the sail caught the wind, how it moved the boat. She carried that knowledge without knowing she would ever need it. Then one day, adrift with twenty-one people on a boat with no engine, that memory surfaced. She gathered scraps of cloth and sewed them into a sail.

It was not training. It was instinct. And behind the instinct was God, who had placed that knowledge inside her for exactly this moment.

She was seventeen when she became captain of the impossible.

She climbed a coconut tree and sat frozen for seven hours without making a sound. She taught frightened strangers a hymn to sing on a drifting boat. She built a raft from sticks and banana stalks and crossed a kilometer of dark water nine times through the night. She nursed a feverish seven-year-old through malaria on an island with no medicine and no shelter.

None of this was asked of her.

What changed inside her during those months was something mothers understand — the moment when the person you love becomes more important than your own survival. Phượng crossed that threshold not for one child but for twenty-one people. She became, without being appointed, the one who kept the group from giving up. The one who stood up in the middle of the chaos and said: we will sing.

She did not do this because she was trained. She did not do this because she was experienced. She did it because God gave her the courage to turn an impossible mission into a possible one — and she was willing to be the vessel.

When I think of faith made visible, I think of my sister Phượng.

She was acting in place of our mother — and our mother would have been proud.

2003, Phượng, Hậu, Hiền, and Mom at Hiền's engagement.

162

Quang Ma

A Tribute To

ÁNH

Ánh was the sibling closest to me after we came to America. In 1983, when he left Vietnam, he carried something none of us fully understood yet — the proof that freedom might actually be possible. His courage became the first light our family had seen in years.

When we heard that Ánh had safely reached Indonesia, relief and longing arrived together. I kept wondering if one day I would see my brother again. At the same time, another thought troubled me: if I failed to escape, would my younger brother, now living abroad, still remember our family? These questions stayed in my mind constantly. Every day I went fishing, and every day I carried a persistent dream — that one day I, too, would leave Vietnam, find freedom, and reunite with him.

That dream became reality only a year later, when I finally saw Ánh again.

After arriving in the United States, I often visited him at the home of Pat and Brian. Ánh and I were meant to stay close — that much was clear from the beginning. During those years, we sometimes worked together — painting houses, repairing walls, doing what needed to be done with our own hands. Before I moved to California, I also stayed at Ánh's house for a time, helping him clean, repair, and renovate the home in Middle Town, NY.

Ánh is someone who willingly opens his home to family and friends almost anytime. He values friendships, enjoys spending time with loved ones, and stays actively involved in church and community activities. His life has always centered around people — building relationships, sharing meals, and creating a warm place where others feel welcome.

He is also the person I have lived closest to and shared the most life experiences with since coming to America. I have learned many good things from Ánh — patience, generosity, and the quiet way he supports others without expecting anything in return.

Through his own experiences, he learned how to navigate challenges in a new country, and he has always been willing to share that wisdom. In many ways, he has paid forward what he learned, helping not only our family but also friends and others who crossed his path.

◆

After living in New York for thirteen years, I was the first in our family to move to the region where I hoped to settle permanently. When I visited Southern California for the first time, I was drawn to the warm sunshine, the open space, and the sense of calm. I told Ánh about it, describing how different it felt from New York. Not long after, he and his wife took a trip to visit San Diego. They quickly fell in love with the area. Three years after I moved, in 2000, they decided to relocate to California as well.

Since then, we have remained close. Every now and then, I drive down to visit him. Sometimes we take his small motorboat out for a few hours of fishing. The steady hum of the engine and the simple conversation between brothers bring back memories of our younger days — the fishing nights in Vietnam when we cooked meals on the boat, surrounded by stars and quiet water, the sky stretching endlessly above us. Those moments remind me that although our lives have changed, the bond between us has remained the same — shaped by shared hardship, strengthened by time, and carried forward with gratitude.

Ánh and I have always helped each other with many projects — installing solar energy, renovating kitchens, fixing homes, and more.

Today we have more than enough, yet we cannot return to those childhood days. Back then, life was poor and difficult. We worked only to earn food for each day. As children, we thought only about survival, but our parents carried much bigger dreams for us. As I grow older, I love and appreciate them even more. No matter what we do, we can never fully repay the love they gave us.

When siblings love and support each other, our parents are happiest. That is one way we can return their love.

He was the first to go.

And because he went first, the rest of us found the courage to follow.

2018 —Ánh with a Big Fish

A Tribute To

THÀNH

Thành was the one who held the helm on the third night, after I had fallen asleep for an hour following the violent, unsettling waves. While the ocean continued to roar around us, he quietly took over, guiding the small wooden boat through the night. In those fragile hours, we relied on each other completely — thirty-nine lives depending on two brothers and the small wooden boat beneath them.

After arriving in America, Thành brought that same steadiness from the boat to his new life. He worked full-time while studying for his GED, pushing himself forward despite exhaustion. Later, he drove a taxi to earn every dollar he could, all while attending college to study aeronautics. Looking back, I believe it came from our parents' deep desire for us to come to America for education. That message reached all of us, and Thành lived it fully.

He eventually settled on the East Coast, and I visit him whenever I can. Throughout his life, he has built many friendships. Social work and charitable acts are at the center of everything he does. During my last visit, I stayed at his house for a few days and witnessed something that deeply moved me.

There were about five additional people living in his home alongside his own family of seven. Some were relatives of his wife, while others were friends of friends. They had come to America struggling to find work and trying to support families back in Vietnam. Feeding twelve mouths was no small thing — yet Thành never made anyone feel like a burden. He allowed them to stay for up to six months, without charging them anything. He helped them search for jobs, guided them through the early challenges, and gave them time to stand on their own feet. Only after they found work did they begin contributing to food and shared expenses.

What he did was something I had never imagined. I realized I might not even be able to do the same myself. His generosity was quiet, natural, and constant.

◆

I also noticed another lesson in the way he raised his children. All four of them became independent soon after high school. They took on small jobs here and there, supporting themselves without relying on their parents. As an uncle, I tried to give them some money during my visit, but they politely refused. At first, I felt a little hurt. Later, I understood. They had been taught not to depend on others. That moment became another lesson I learned from Thành — not only generosity, but also independence.

Reflecting on this, I was reminded of our father. He never kept money for himself. Whatever he earned, he often sent back to Vietnam to support relatives in need. From our parents, we learned that true happiness comes more from giving than from receiving.

Thành held the helm that third night so I could rest.

He has never stopped holding it.

And looking back across all the years — from that fragile wooden boat on the open sea to the home full of strangers

Thành welcomed without hesitation — I believe He was there through all of it. Not only watching over our uncertain journeys from ocean to land, but guiding our lives long after we reached the shore. Every act of courage, every quiet generosity, every open door — none of it was ours alone.

Someone above was holding the helm too.

Epilogue

FAITH THAT CARRIED US HOME

This story does not end with escape.

It ends with the faith that carried us home.

As the years passed, I came to see that every step of our journey was held together by something stronger than any boat, any raft, or any human plan: faith.

My mother suffered most of all. She watched her children leave one by one, each goodbye a small death. She lived with unanswered questions, wondering whether they were still alive, whether the sea or jungle had claimed them. When Phượng and Út escaped by land through Cambodia and Thailand, she waited five long months before hearing they were safe. For most of that time there was no news at all. Unable to stay still, she traveled to Cambodia herself, following rumors, asking strangers, hoping for any sign. She returned empty-handed, her heart heavy with grief. Only after five months did the news arrive. Her joy was beyond words.

Looking back, I understand that none of her suffering was unseen. Every sleepless night, every tear, every whispered prayer was known to God.

"Thou tellest my wanderings: put thou my tears into thy bottle: are they not in thy book?" (Psalm 56:8)

Those words describe my mother perfectly. God counted every tear she cried while waiting for her children. Only now do I truly understand the Vietnamese saying: "A mother's heart is as vast as the peaceful ocean."

Mom, 2004. Her faith was the anchor that held us all.

And even greater than a mother's love is God's promise:

"Can a woman forget her sucking child, that she should not have compassion on the son of her womb? Yea, they may forget yet will I not forget thee." (Isaiah 49:15)

My mother never forgot us. And through faith, she trusted God would not forget us either.

It was faith that kept my father steady at the wheel during those fourteen days adrift, when death felt closer than land.

It was faith that gave Phượng the courage to climb a coconut tree and sit silent for seven hours while pirates raged below.

It was faith that carried me through failing grades, lonely nights, and the long drives between Las Vegas and Redlands, when love and exhaustion pulled in opposite directions.

It was faith that whispered to my parents in the flooded fields of Đồng Tháp Mười: one day, your children will stand together, free.

We did not survive because we were stronger or smarter than the storms. We survived because we were never alone. God walked with us across oceans, through jungles, and into refugee camps. He placed kind strangers in our path — Brian and Pat Carew, Elizabeth the teacher, Mr. S., Hùng, the college friend who made one life-changing phone call possible. He turned despair into small miracles: a hose of fresh water from a passing ship, a wooden lid that fit perfectly, a diploma held in trembling hands while family watched from the front row.

Today, our family is scattered but whole. We live in different states, with different careers and different dreams. Yet we are bound by the same thread that once felt so fragile: the faith that carried us home.

To anyone reading these words who feels their own life hanging by a thread — take heart. The storms will come. The nights will feel endless. But faith is not the absence of fear; it is the courage to keep going through it. And on the other side of every storm, there is something waiting — something that can heal, restore, and make all things new.

I no longer wonder if the dream was worth the price.

I know it was.

And I know it still is.

With endless gratitude.

ACKNOWLEDGMENTS

For more than forty years, these memories lived quietly inside me. They waited.

I often told myself that one day I would write this book — not only to remember, but to leave something real behind for my son Andrew and for the children of my brothers and sisters. This is the story of where we came from, what we endured, and what survival truly cost.

This book exists because of many people who, in different ways, encouraged me, supported me, and believed in me.

I would like to express my heartfelt gratitude to the crew of the Norwegian ship Essy Silje, who turned back on May 11, 1984, and rescued thirty-nine refugees from the South China Sea after spotting our small drifting boat. They are the reason this book exists at all.

First and above all, I thank my parents. Your courage, sacrifice, and unwavering faith shaped not only my survival but my entire life. Everything I have become rests on the foundation you built under circumstances few people can truly imagine.

To my mother, whose love, strength, and endurance carried our family through years of uncertainty and separation. Your faith sustained us long before we understood the depth of what you endured.

To my siblings, who shared the same fragile beginnings, the same fears, and the same uncertain journey. Our bond will always remain unbreakable.

To my wife Julie, who has walked beside me through the many seasons of our life together and stood faithfully by my side while I wrote this story. Your love has been my safe harbor.

To my son Andrew, whose persistence, patience, and steady belief gave me the courage to finally write this story. Without your encouragement, these pages might never have been written.

To Brian and Pat Carew, who opened their home and their hearts to our family when America was still new and strange. Brian has since passed, but his kindness lives on in these pages and in our hearts. Pat, thank you for being family.

To my friends and colleagues who listened with open hearts — thank you for helping me transform private memories into something I could share.

And finally, to every refugee, every boat person, and every family who has carried their past across dangerous waters. This book is written in your honor. I share it with a grateful heart.

ABOUT THE AUTHOR

Quang Ma was born in Vietnam and came of age during one of the most turbulent periods in the country's history. In the aftermath of the Fall of Saigon, his childhood was shaped by displacement, hardship, and the lasting impact of war. His family's journey — marked by perilous escapes by sea and by land, years of separation, and an eventual reunion — left a profound imprint on his life and faith.

After arriving in the United States, Quang rebuilt his future through perseverance, education, and a deep commitment to service. He pursued a career in pharmacy and has spent the past fifteen years serving patients at the Loma Linda VA Medical Center, where he continues to care for veterans while mentoring and training pharmacy residents. His work reflects the same resilience, discipline, and sense of purpose that carried him through his earliest years.

Life Hanging by a Thread is his first book. More than a memoir, it is a testimony of faith, endurance, and the sacrifices that shaped his family's journey to freedom. Through this story, Quang hopes to honor those who did not survive and offer hope to anyone whose own life feels like it is hanging by a thread.

Quang lives in the United States with his wife, Julie, and their son, Andrew. His life stands as a reflection not only of survival, but of faith, gratitude, and the enduring belief that even the most fragile thread can lead to a new beginning.

*Our lives once hung by a thread—
but faith carried us all the way home. My friends call me Captain Q
—a quiet reminder of the small boat that once carried us toward
freedom.*
*"Crossing the Long Night Sea" A song written by the
author, inspired by this journey. Listen at:*
https://suno.com/s/bU1KwpeVUWfoGAuD

May God bless you and your family on your own journey of faith, hope, and perseverance.

If this story touched you, I would be grateful if you would consider leaving an honest review on Amazon. Your feedback helps others discover this journey and means more than you know.

Thank you for reading—and for sharing in this journey.

For permission requests or inquiries, please contact:

lifehangingbyathread@yahoo.com

www.ingramcontent.com/pod-product-compliance
Lightning Source LLC
Chambersburg PA
CBHW060540160726
47991CB00001B/406